Creativity in STEM Fields

A View from an Eclectic Mind

Malgorzata Marciniak, PhD

ALINEA

Alinea Learning

Boston

ALINEA

Alinea Learning
Boston, Massachusetts
Published in the United States by Alinea Learning,
an imprint and division of Alinea Knowledge, LLC, Boston.

Visit our website at www.alinealearning.com.

Library of Congress Cataloging-in-Publication Data is available on file.

Print book ISBN: 979-8-9892140-2-0

eBook ISBN: 979-8-9892140-3-7

Cover design by Imprudent Press LLC

Cover copyright © 2024 by Alinea Knowledge, LLC

This book is dedicated to everyone who taught me to be creative, even if they did it in non-creative ways.

'I daresay you haven't had much practice,' said the Queen. 'When I was your age, I always did it for half-an-hour a day. Why, sometimes I've believed as many as six impossible things before breakfast [...]'

"Alice in Wonderland" by Lewis Carroll

vii

Preface

That day, February 19, 2020, when I attended a lecture and a concert at the Julliard School of Music with a friend, remains in my memory. Nothing could have made me happier than experiencing both venues, a music concert and a research lecture together. Interestingly, I don't remember the concert, but the lecture focused on the neuroscience of creativity, with musicians as the subjects of the research. Classical musicians were compared to improvising musicians using fMRI scans. After the lecture, I spoke with the presenter, requested a copy of the paper (Chan Barrett & Limb, 2019) via Research Gate, and read it carefully on the same day. The idea of scanning creative brains impressed me greatly, and while passionately discussing its implications with a friend, I decided to write a book about creativity in STEM fields. As a researcher of creativity, I could not miss such a chance of being inspired to do something new from something old.

This volume aims to show STEM instructors a path for introducing creativity in the college and possibly high school curriculum. This work is directed to university faculty of math courses and high school teachers interested in developing their creative skills and bringing elements of creative assignments to their classrooms. This work may be particularly valuable for teachers of non-traditional students who would like to find a way to teach every student individually while encouraging group activities and collaboration. College and high school students may benefit from absorbing the concepts laid out here and expanding them for their purposes.

This volume seeks to fill the gap in the existing literature and addresses the need to carry creativity in STEM in collegial education. This work is based on my first-hand experience as a researcher in a community college. I have focused my class activities on incorporating creative research projects into the college curriculum in the classroom and outside. Amazed by the different attitudes displayed by students while working on research-oriented projects that contained creative elements, I decided to incorporate creative projects in my classrooms. This placed me on the path of discovery of my own creativity, which sparked my enthusiasm for pedagogical work. This changed how I teach, think, work, and research. This changed the way I live. Most importantly, emphasizing creativity shifted the importance of learning from learning a particular subject of mathematics to incorporating that subject among previously learned subjects, making a fine mind structure.

We all need to be creative daily to move our reality towards progress. The education that we are offering today should reflect the fast-changing digital era we are currently living in. Today, science and technology are growing faster than ever, supported by analyzing terabytes of data that can fit on a tiny device. It does not take much to understand that we simply cannot predict the future needs of our students. That is why we should teach them how to be creative and hope that this little knowledge they learn at school gives them a basis for further growth.

It is important to understand that only a teacher who treasures a creative thought can successfully teach creativity to students. Thus, before preparing the first creative class assignments, the initial stages of the path contain self-awakening of creative thoughts within topics not necessarily well known to the reader. May the path to creative thought begin for the reader with the purpose of re-shaping college education.

I would like to study various paths of awakening creativity among readers for future research. So, stay tuned to yourself since I want to hear from you and learn how you made it into the creative side of your mind. Please send the report with the answers to book questions, your comments, and reflections on the process to my email address, malgorzata.aneta.marciniak@gmail.com, with the subject line: Creativity in STEM fields.

For whom is the book written? Initially, I had college and high school teachers in mind because I was familiar with the challenges of this group. However, in the process of writing, a colleague of mine suggested expanding the audience to include college and high school students. After giving this idea a few thoughts, I have realized that open-minded students may benefit from this book just as much as their teachers, or maybe even more. Moreover, the students will carry their wisdom into the future, to which I do not have access. Thus, I will take students' presence in the audience as an extension of this idea to the future.

I often ask myself to be more specific and visualize those teachers and students to whom the book may be addressed. When I close my eyes, I see those who really need to uncover or discover their creative vibes to improve their daily routines or the quality of their internal dialog.

Thus, I imagine teachers who go to class and apply their heart to teaching and are deeply moved by the observation that students are not learning.

The book also has in mind a student who wants to expand their learning beyond the school curriculum and beyond the conventional educational paradigms. This process is particularly painful in traditional mathematics classrooms, where mathematical ways of thinking are imposed without giving any reasoning or any inquiry. What are the reasons for this shortage of creativity in the math classroom? Or is it not only math and school but something more fundamental? This question may require some elaborate reflections. Rollo May in his book "The courage to create" (May R. , 1975) points out that the shortage of creativity has its roots in a basic fear of discovering the truth about one's nature. However, at the same time, it is dangerous to discover the gaps in reality created by one's family, job, town community, or the entire society and the government. Add social media, a group of friends, or coworkers to discover that in every stage of individual growth and evolutionary growth of the human population, someone is imposing some view of reality on others. Moreover, others were imposing on someone. This mental inbreeding is very visible in the mentalities of little towns or small societies, where a small click of individuals mirrors each other's frame of mind, narrowing it with every step. I always thought the problem with the shortage of creativity was in the minds' laziness and obedience to accepting well-traveled paths. However, now I see that this view is a mere oversimplification. The survival mechanism prefers a delicate balance between obedience to the group reality, creative vibes imposed by necessity, and a sense of wonder. Rollo May discusses the intensity of the encounter of creative vibrations. He points out that in the blunt realm of daily routines, the moments of creative insight shine like diamonds. They carry the power to erase bad memories and the power to heal anxiety, trauma, and accumulation of disappointments. In a search for sparks, I keep trying and going from one project to another, never satisfied and never filled, always hungry and always searching for more and beyond. However, what may appear to be a monkey mind is more like a driving force, a consistent and persistent desire to expand and grow the mindset beyond and beyond the sea of known. When the mind becomes temporarily filled with content, it must write or speak, or it will blow up, collapse, and then resume after a moment of decay. Sounds familiar? Rollo May discusses the necessity of alternating between work and relaxation to encourage creative energy. In the middle of profoundly engaging work, take a break and relax; in the middle of relaxation, dive into the burning questions of why and how. Who would have expected this little book by Rollo May, which I picked up randomly at the Graduate Center library, to prove so insightful? Moreover, I cannot believe my reasoning for choosing this book, not another book, was silly. I got it because it simply fits in my tiny purse, and I could read it on the subway. Small is beautiful! Coincidentally, Rollo May quotes Poincare (Poincaré, 1914) to justify why this and no other ideas are picked from the vastness of the subconscious mind, giving an argument for beauty. I would add the saying that beauty is in the eye of the observer, meaning that out of the unbounded, one's consciousness picks those messages that are somehow tuned to it or fit in the opening. It may be an answer to a burning question or an idea that solves a disturbing problem. Alternatively, he roughly pretends to do that with a certain approximation. Here, we are examining the challenging aspects of creativity in STEM fields. They all have the same features; they are far from "natural" inquiries of the human mind that revolve around the state of the heart of daily routines or the beings around. Giving an example from mathematics, most math inquiries are buried underneath mathematical notation, terminology, and previous discoveries of generations of mathematicians. Thus, the opening for mathematical discoveries must be skillfully and consistently encouraged as it will not likely appear spontaneously in most minds.

The book is structured in the following way:

After a chapter on motivation, there are chapters about the definition of the stages of creativity, as in Wallas (Wallas, 1926) and Csikszentmihalyi (Csikszentmihalyi, 1974). The examples assist the definitions of stages. Chapter 3 contains a creative dispute regarding the position of creativity in Bloom's taxonomy. Chapter 4 consists mainly of developmental theories for children's growth, according to Piaget (Piaget, 1952) and Vygotsky (Vygotsky, 1978), and for the mind organization of adults, according to Kegan (Kegan, 1982). Since I did not imagine that teachers who do not facilitate their creativity could successfully facilitate it in the classroom, thus some advice on self-development of creativity is presented in Chapter 5. Chapter 6 contains ideas for research projects for various subjects, while Chapter 7 includes sample classroom assignments. Ideas for assessment, inspired by the Torrent Test, are in Chapter 8. Since reflections are very important for the growth of creativity, chapter 9 includes reflections from the times of the pandemic, which, in my opinion, tested the capacity of the teachers for creative ways. Chapter 10 consists of reflections on the path and possible ideas for future work. Each chapter is assisted by a suitable picture among paintings traditionally attributed to Tenshō Shūbun (天章周文) (1414-1463) and verses by Kuòān Shīyuǎn; translation by Senzaki Nyogen (千崎如幻) (1876–1958) and Paul Reps (1895-1990), https://en.wikipedia.org/wiki/Ten_Bulls

In Search of the Bull

In the pasture of the world,
I endlessly push aside the tall
grasses in search of the Ox.
Following unnamed rivers,
lost upon the interpenetrating
paths of distant mountains,
My strength failing and my vitality exhausted, I cannot find the Ox.

—1—

Can Creativity be Taught and Learned?

This chapter is dedicated to those who may doubt whether STEM education can accommodate creative activities. I will explain whether creativity may be taught and learned in the classroom. In my opinion, creativity can be facilitated and, if encouraged, may flourish. Facilitation of creativity does not guarantee that everybody in a classroom will arrive at some creative ideas, but it opens space for some students to develop creative thought.

When asked about the factors contributing to success in math classes, my students frequently mention talent as the most important. Similarly, it is expected to think that someone is or is not creative, and creativity does not significantly vary throughout someone's life. While an instant transformation from an entirely non-creative mind to impulsively creative does not sound realistic, a gradual work on the skills, the subject of this volume, is possible. Since working with the students' minds is a daily activity for all teachers, I am proposing gradual changes to more creative approaches. Due to the plasticity of the mind (Marzenic, 2013) this task can be accomplished.

Evolutionary necessity

Regardless of popular stereotypes about the need for creative vibes during human evolution, I suspect that creativity has been a necessary skill since the inception of humankind. That is probably because fate is inventive in bringing unexpected circumstances and new challenges. Even in our highly predicted daily routines, the next day is not a mere copy of the previous day, always carrying something new. Going one step deeper into the reflections about the need for creativity in daily life, one can state that creativity has been the sole property of the human mind. One may inquire whether it enters the minds of other species since they also experience challenges and caprices of nature. It is true that monkeys and certain birds use tools (sticks or stones) to open nuts. Moreover, they can indeed teach their offspring such skills. However, do they reflect on the process of creation or teaching to such an extent as we humans do? I will claim that creativity is a unique property of the human mind and significantly contributes to the evolutionary success of our species. It seems that for the survival and well-being of human society, not everybody needs to be highly creative since just a few individuals make spectacular creations. However, the truth is that we all are performing small creative acts daily, often not even fully realizing them. Creativity is not only the activity reserved for the learned, the artists, the poets, or the engineers. It is a common thing to be creative. However, being aware of the creative process and being able to improve one's creative skills are more subtle. Hopefully, this volume will help build such awareness by offering insight into developing the process of self-improvement to introduce creativity in a college or high school STEM classroom.

In 1964, Kuhn formulated a theory of scientific revolutions (Kuhn, 2012), which briefly can be described as alternating gradual and rapid changes in the growth of sciences. Moreover, Kuhn emphasized the incommensurability of the quality of accomplishments performed within the frames of different paradigms. It is worth noting that revolutionary changes are not exclusive to political or socio-economic human history or the growth of sciences but are frequently observed in nature as giant stellar collisions or mass extinctions of species on Earth. Multiple attempts have been made to dispute, modify, or generalize the original idea of scientific revolutions, for example, in education. In the light of that concept, Ellis and Berry (Ellis & Berry III, 2005) discussed the paradigm shifts in mathematics education in the USA related to what is meaningful in mathematics and how it should be tested.

What is significant is that the past pivoting moments were happening more sparsely, with the spans of 60-80 years for the times of secular or compulsory education or 10-20 years for the times of "New Math" and "No Child Behind Act." However, the two revolutionary changes that took place very recently, the pandemic and the appearance of chatbots, happened close to one another. The pandemic that lasted worldwide roughly between March 2020 and March 2022 was created by nature. The appearance of an advanced chatbot took place in November 2022 and was entirely developed by humans. Since all things in the universe are inevitably connected, there is a possibility that the extended time of the pandemic put a sprout on the appearance of advanced chatbots due to the excessive spare time of researchers or hiring a larger than usual number of programmers simultaneously. Based on that observation, one can conclude that due to the accelerated speed of growth of technology and human development, paradigm shifts will take place more frequently in the future than in the past. This will affect the shape of education and impose a strain on educators. Education must reformulate some of its paradigms to accommodate the expected changes and the frequent

3

appearances of pivoting moments. Without revisions, education will become outdated and eventually reduced (just like other unaligned things in nature), marking the beginning of the end of our civilization. Thus, creativity in education is an evolutionary necessity.

Can Creativity Spark the Experience of Mathematics?

Why should we even attempt to teach students some entirely useless skills? Unfortunately, that is how math students (and teachers) often feel. The rigid formalism of mathematics is considered the highest accomplishment of generations of mathematicians, and their work across the globe and throughout centuries has become the curse of the school subject. This rigor of mathematics exposition became a nightmare for students and a source of anxiety for many. Where does the anxiety come from? How often did teachers hear from students that they studied for the entire night, and everything disappeared from their memory while taking an exam? Similarly, students usually claim that they know how to add and multiply numbers, but they cannot execute these rules correctly every time.

While many teachers may not believe in the honesty of these statements, I do believe them since I have experienced similar symptoms. It is not uncommon for me to forget everything when I am emotional. Being angry or hurried suddenly erases my memory of facts and skills. Trying to do calculations after being punched in the nose will not likely lead to the correct results. This strategy of the mind in a dangerous situation of emptying itself from all irrelevant knowledge is an evolutionary function. This helped our ancestors think quickly and clearly to survive, but the same strategy applied during a vital exam may lead to a complete failure. Thus, a frustrated student who fears that during a quiz they will likely forget everything learned the previous day.

4

I remember a research meeting with two skillful and experienced colleagues when we were sitting in a coffee shop and solving math problems from our research seminar. We arrived at the point where we had to perform specific calculations requiring basic algebraic skills. However, the level of complexity of the expressions was so high that we spent the entire hour before we agreed on the results. Then we confirmed it with software, laughing at ourselves and our sloppiness, but this made me think that knowing the rules and consistently applying them correctly is not the same. Should we then grade math students for perfect correctness of their calculations? If not, then how should we grade them? Are there other ways to assess students' progress? Can modern education use them in determining students' course grades?

However, shall we drop entirely the arithmetic skills of applying basic rules over and over and rigorously executing them? In my understanding, a person who cannot follow basic rules of addition and multiplication should not be expected to perform skillfully on other tasks of modern life, such as following the Traffic Laws, Tax Rules, or Voting Policies. A giant metropolis such as New York City has complicated rules to follow daily, and even using a subway pass requires specific skills of following the guidelines carefully. Some may argue that mathematics is boring and that doing meaningless calculations with no purpose or goal is tedious. Moreover, I agree that students' interest, involvement, and enthusiasm can give meaning to any subject. Thus, motivating involvement has been a challenge for generations of teachers all over the globe. However, improving students' involvement in math classes remains an unsolved problem in its full generality.

In my classes, students frequently request applications of mathematical concepts that appear in class. However, when the time of the test comes, they beg for not having those application problems on the test. After realizing that pattern, I concluded that in math courses for engineers, there is a vast selection of engineering students who do not feel comfortable with applications from other areas of engineering. Thus, civil engineering students strongly object to applications with circuits, and electrical engineering students despise applications in statistics. To resolve that issue, I have introduced applied projects in my classes, where students can select their favorite topics or create their projects. In my understanding this technique improves both, students' involvement and creativity.

Is a STEM classroom a good place to (re)learn creativity?

While visualizing a creative person, we may have in mind an image of an individual artist (or a scientist) going through creative processes in the solitary atelier. Still, discussions with peers and their suggestions, appreciation, or words of criticism are crucial in a creative process. In other words, in creativity, "no man is an island entire of itself." I recall that many interesting research conclusions were revealed during interactions with others. My most enlightening observations arrived when I was observing others, for example, my students, who were going through creative processes. These observations proved to me the significance of a social experience of creativity. I think the intensity of the creative process experience may be so absorbing that self-reflection and self-observation may be limited. Thus, observing others during that process may be a crucial aspect in the growth of self-awareness of one's creativity. That is why, in my classes and during research meetings, I encourage students to work in groups and share their experiences related to their thinking processes. In my understanding, we often imitate and later adapt the new skills of the mind after observing them in the others. Thus, learning the skill of creativity in a classroom may be improved by collective experience shared by groups of peers. This aspect of creative work should not involve competing with others but can contain nonjudgmental comparisons of the stages of the creative processes among the researchers. This aspect of

6

creative work should solely focus on building awareness and sensitivity to the creative signals. I believe that the social experiences of the creative process may be a natural way to grow creative awareness since humans tend to be highly sociable creatures who enrich each other through encouragement and shared experiences. My impressions are supported by research in neuroscience related to mirror neurons (Ramachandran, 1995).

The role of mirror neurons in experiencing creativity in a group

Mirror neurons were discovered in 1992 by Giacomo Rizzolatti and a group of researchers in Parma, Italy. They have the property of firing when one performs an action and when one observes that action being performed by others. (Keysers, Kaas, & Gazzola, 2010). Even if the role of mirror neurons remains disputable among neuroscientists (Taylor, 2016) this discovery leads to various hypotheses about the possible roles of the mirror neurons in cognitive processes, particularly creativity.

Following the concept of the "imitative" function of mirror neurons (Pineda, 2009), one may inquire about their roles in the processes and flows of creativity. Claiming that mirror neurons play a role in a learning process supports the idea that while teaching the material, we also teach our students some mental processes and attitudes connected to it. For example, our love of mathematics may be contagious and spread out to some individuals. Thus, we should expect that once exposed to other individuals experiencing creative cycles and flow, our students have increased chances of experiencing such a flow independently.

I wholeheartedly support the idea that observing others while they experience creative processes is of excellent value to the observer. That is because my interest in creativity was initiated by my observations when working with students on creative research problems. I realized that

7

students behaved differently and carried different attitudes when working in my office on creative math problems than when they worked in a classroom on mundane assignments. I have no doubts that this curiosity, which grew in me over time, was detached from self-awareness and entirely rooted in observing my students. In my understanding, there is a lot to research about the role of the influences of social experiences on the creativity of individuals.

Practice of experiencing creativity in a group

The pandemic sometimes gave me surprising insight into creativity. I discovered that the group does not have to meet in person for the individuals to experience the power of mirror neurons. The excitement and enthusiasm can be passed across space and time without losing intensity. We all experience it while reading an exciting book written by a person passionate about their work and discoveries. Modern technology and its vast availability of free networking make sharing more accessible than ever. In my classes, when introducing assignments for creative projects, I frequently use examples of work performed by students from previous semesters. For the first time, when presenting the projects in the classroom, I used an example of students' work from a mentored research project. Usually, I display the slides and show a video pointing out what is valuable and significant about students' presentations. For example, recently, my students in the Differential Equations class found articles about designing loops of roller coasters and prepared a quality presentation with a historical background and multiple details related to various designs of the loops. Finding a topic was a creative assignment since students read the guidelines and reflected on their interests, connecting them with the material learned in the classroom. This presentation will be shown to students next semester as an example of an excellent choice of topic. It will encourage students to search for something exciting. Students who prepared the presentation about rollercoasters wrote in their self-report about creativity:

"After doing a significant amount of research, our group had a blast learning more about how these attractions worked, more specifically, the loop aspect of the rollercoasters. It would be insane to see how these engineers create other inversions that are more complicated than the shape of these loops. The concepts used in this project mainly came from physics, but it was cool to see differential equations take a role in helping determine the shape of the loop itself. This project also was an eye-opener to show us that these engineers must work carefully as they are responsible for the lives of people that dare to embrace the thrill."

An attentive observer could see that one student infected others with his idea, and they got excited about it just as much as he did.

Creating groups based on a diversity of skills

Often, as teachers, we struggle and complain about the body of students in the classroom being highly diverse in terms of students' preparation, dedication, and skill levels. I can relate to it and agree that the homogeneity of the classroom makes lectures more aligned with students' needs. However, in the case of creative assignments, the situation is quite opposite. Diversity in a group offers a chance to exchange the results of creative assignments and the entire creative thinking process with its errors, reflections, and corrections. Thus, I encourage students to collaborate based on diversity while facilitating creative assignments.

This aspect of work is closely related to experiencing creativity in a group but focuses on experiencing it within a non-homogenous group. At the beginning of the semester, my students receive a sheet with self-assessment questions about their level of skills: math, language, collaboration, and public speaking. Bringing these particular skill categories is justified by my observations and assessments from previous semesters. In my classes, students may represent highly varied levels of math skills due to their diverse backgrounds. In addition, some students return to college after a long absence and may not feel comfortable with all studying skills. Reading, writing, and public speaking are categories motivated by the fact that a significant percentage of the student body consists of non-native speakers. The range may be ample, containing students who just arrived from abroad and, for example, can read and write excellently but have serious difficulties speaking English. Some students may have completed American high school, but English is not their first language, and they do not use it daily. These students may lack some language skills but be firm in others. During the semester, students are encouraged to observe these skills among other students and attempt to compose their project teams based on the complementarity of the skills, not on friendships, race, gender, or such.

I have observed that students with creative ideas either prepare the projects independently or compose their project teams easily according to their own needs. However, students who do not have innovative ideas and were not chosen to complete someone's team struggle with decisions about their topic and have difficulties delivering a quality presentation in a timely manner.

To support my students' collaborative skills, I mention in class that the most valuable creative environment is formed by the free flow of information among researchers representing various areas of expertise and multiple levels of insight. While working with students on mentored research projects, I found their naïve attitude particularly valuable. As I noticed, students often try to work on exciting ideas. At the same time, professors' expertise and experience of previous unsuccessful work on such ideas made us lean toward the direction of accessible problems. This dual approach usually places the team within the scope of exciting projects that are workable and publishable, not only conversational for a theory or hypothesis.

The role of the teacher

How much should the teacher be involved in the creative process? In my understanding, it is sufficient to show students how to start the project and then influence the work as little as possible, ensuring that students enjoy the process and keep progressing in understanding and growing creativity.

At the same time, I do not visualize someone without excessive experience in the creative process trying to facilitate such a process for others. Working on my research and doing creative artwork significantly improves my skills as a facilitator of the creative abilities of others, in this case, students in my classes and students who work on research projects with me. To summarize my experience with creative assignments within the curriculum and beyond, I would say that everyone needs to find a unique way of implementing creativity in their work and daily life.

Classroom creativity supported by brief creative assignments

This momentary experience of creative thought can be facilitated in a classroom even with little time and equally little effort from a trained teacher. A brief assignment is supposed to be short in preparation, quick in performance, ungraded, or low stakes. Students should not feel that they are evaluated or judged during such assignments. But even a light smile or a teacher's blink may reveal to the students the accuracy of their answers. The primary purpose of brief creative assignments is to provide a feeling of immediate response, which cannot be incorrect. That is why it is good to focus on how students think rather than what they produce. Examples of brief assignments can be given at the beginning of each topic when students do not know and are not supposed to know the correct answers. They are not expected to display a proper way of thinking but to wander around the idea randomly and report on what comes to their mind based on free associations. The reward of a diverse classroom is that students can compare their possibly incorrect answers to gain a view into other students' minds. Reflecting on a comparison of these answers provides insight that is unavailable to lone learners. It is always rewarding to have sequences of such brief assignments to, for example, justify why a uniform notation is necessary in mathematics.

Classroom creativity supported by research projects

It is a real challenge to match students with topics. The topics for my favorite project (Geometry of Solar Panels) were determined based on informal discussions among students and me. The story began when two of my classes were scheduled consecutively in the same room where I would stay during the break. Somehow, two of my students would come early to class and chat with me there. This way, we developed favorable initial conditions for free time and uninterrupted conversation space. Starting with very casual topics about neighborhood coffee shops, we swiftly shifted to our favorite books and movies, followed by what we would like to work on. One student mentioned that she would like to work on a project connecting the calculus she learned at college and her passion for civil engineering and architecture. She wondered whether wrapping an entire building with flexible transparent solar panels would be reasonable. I responded that it would be very wasteful because the position of the panels toward the sun determines its efficiency. Thus, the part facing north may not be as efficient as in other directions. We wanted to determine which shapes are efficient and how to position flexible solar panels toward the sun for the best efficiency. Later, those students became the best advertisers for my projects and classes. Walking around the college and displaying their enthusiasm related to learning mathematics in the context of research projects, they convinced other students to do the same. Many students walk into my office to inquire about the possibility of working on projects together and often report that they do not expect research projects to be offered at a community college. This shows the necessity of a specific advertisement for the research projects.

Discovery of the Footprints

Along the riverbank, under the trees,
I discover footprints.
Even under the fragrant grass,
I see his prints.
Deep in remote mountains, they are found.
These traces can no more be hidden
than one's nose, looking heavenward.

—2—

Definitions and Stages

The way creativity is defined for our purposes may shape the entire presentation, so it is reasonable to spend a few paragraphs thinking about what we understand by creativity. From the point of view of education, creativity may be defined differently than it is defined from a professionals' point of view. An artist, a poet, a scientist, or an engineer sees creativity through their territory of activities, but a teacher sees creativity as their own or students' experience. Creativity from a student's perspective may be even more enigmatic since students on the path of education are usually not exposed to the newest world-class research. Here, the theoretical topics of definitions and stages are kept to a minimum; for more details, one can consider Chapter 1 in (Chamberlin, Liljedahl, & Savich, 2022).

What is Creativity?

In simple words, creativity happens when something new is made from something old. This may apply to new ideas, applications of previously known methods or devices, modifications, or generalizations of previously known methods or devices to fit new applications. Sometimes, creativity may be understood as "problem-solving." However, for education, this may be misleading when solving a problem, which may not require creating new thoughts but is a mere compilation of previously mastered methods. Frequently, students with a good memory for learning methods are considered gifted in mathematics while not displaying creativity in that direction. Focusing solely on the appearance of the solution to a problem prepared by such a student, one may not be able to recognize whether the methods were previously learned or whether the student is performing an act of creation.

When working on a piece of artwork, artists may not solve well defined problems (like we do in STEM), but they are still considered creative. Leaving behind various aspects of artistic creativity, a working definition of creativity for education may be formulated as follows: creativity takes place when someone, using known components, brings suggestions for giving them a new meaning and is involved in improving or debating such design. This touches upon the composite nature of things and the reflective aspects of the creative process. Especially in STEM fields, creative work does not happen in one step but is improved during a process that alternates reflections and practice. It sounds obvious, but it may be worth emphasizing that those components are known to the performer. This is usually not the case at school, where creativity is supposed to support learning, not replace it. Thus, the "known components" of a new creation are, in fact, the subjects of learning. Similarly, when we say that in a creative process, something new is obtained, it may be wise to mention that this "new thing" is indeed new to the performer. Since there is no way

16

to verify in an objective way that something is entirely new in the universe, the school version of "new" is modified to "new to the student." Here is a new, more precise version of the creative process and creativity containing previously mentioned elements.

Creativity is the process of trials and reflections when something new to the student is made from something that is known or is in the process of learning.

However, the definition of creativity formulated this way does not touch upon the most crucial aspect of the creative process. Thus, it will be reformulated after introducing the concept of the subconscious.

Some light on the stages of creativity

In his book "The Art of Thought" Graham Wallas (Wallas, 1926) underlines the necessity of observing the thinking process while learning the actual subject (page 28):

"But behind the use of thinkers of rules and materials drawn from the sciences, there has always been, since the dawn of civilization, an unformulated 'mystery' of thought which has been 'explained' by no science and has been independently discovered, lost, and rediscovered, by successive creative thinkers. [Who] learnt from each other something which was neither logic nor accumulated knowledge."

This "mystery" from the quote above describes connections between subconscious and conscious mental formations generated during learning and outside of it. Wallas indicates four stages of thought: Preparation stage, Incubation stage, Illumination stage, and Verification stage. In short, the Preparation stage occurs when a student learns about the problem. The Incubation stage happens when the subconscious mind is working on the inquiry. The most mysterious stage is the Illumination stage, where the subconscious mind reveals its findings to the conscious mind and brings them to the student's attention. The Verification stage occurs when the conscious mind analyzes the provided results with the conscious mind and verifies the results. However, this is only a brief glimpse of the stages; they are much more complicated and mysterious than meet the eye. Moreover, one observes that problem-solving consists of multiple repetitions of those four stages. Indeed, anybody who has ever solved a fundamental problem knows that the first solution provided by the subconscious mind may be incorrect or incomplete, and the entire process becomes more of a cycle, where collecting information and incubating the answers, then illuminating them, and eventually revealing to the conscious mind, follow one another multiple times. An example of such a sequence encouraged by a mentor is, for example, revealed in "Minutes from math meetings with an undergraduate student" (Marciniak M. A., 2017) The focused state that involves those stages was already recognized and described as Creative Flow by Csikszentmihalyi (Csikszentmihalyi, 1974).

Conscious vs Subconscious

What is relevant is that the Preparation and Verification stages occur primarily in the conscious mind while the Incubation occurs in the subconscious mind. The Illumination stage relies on the connection between those two aspects. Since we have awareness in the conscious states, grasping them is not a mystery. The conscious mind holds short-term memory, awareness, critical thinking, logical thinking, or willpower. However, the subconscious is more challenging to explain and (indirectly) observe. The subconscious mind holds long-term memory, intuition, imagination, emotions, habits, values, beliefs, or sense of existence. Pictorial representation of the conscious and the subconscious mind resembles the iceberg, with the small tip above the water representing the conscious mind. Most mental processes occur "underneath the waters" in the subconscious mind.

Here are some reflections related to the stages of creative thought in the context of the classroom and beyond.

Preparation

This is when the information is placed in someone's attention, and memorized sufficiently to make connections to later retrieve it during the other stages. At first, this stage may seem very simple and has low relevance, but this stage is the key to other stages. Its mystery is not about what material is being memorized but how it is assisted by subconscious impulses, which may trigger connections with other topics later. Memorizing in the classroom may be limited to just the basic external senses: vision, hearing, touching, or less recognized in the classroom, the senses of smell, taste, or feeling. When I ask my students which senses they use while learning mathematics, they predominantly mention vision and hearing. However, at the same time, when we entered an overly cold (or overly heated) or smelly classroom, they refused to stay for a lesson. Can you imagine trying to learn calculus while being tickled or having toothache? The sense of feeling can generate exigent distractions. How about the sense of taste? Did you ingest a certain number of sugary drinks, sweets, or other comforting foods to calm yourself down before an exam or after some particularly unpleasant activity? It may happen someday that before math classes, we will intentionally hand students a piece of cake to reduce anxiety and make their learning experience more pleasant. This stage of Preparation is about bringing something new to the conscious mind with the assistance of some subconscious associations. It is essential that the students enjoy the subject, like the teacher, like their colleagues, and feel comfortable in the school environment. Whether they feel comfortable in their chair or disturbed by their internal feelings and thoughts. Here comes the most critical revelation. This preparation stage may not be as dependent on external factors as we imagine but may be more dependent on the internal attitudes of the students. The most crucial factor may be excitement about the topic and the entire learning process.

Preparation may also occur when students work on their homework assignments or have doubts about solutions and develop ideas for solving them. Ask your students and yourself about the best and most memorable ways to acquire knowledge. Is it during a lecture? Homework? Discussion? What are the favorite features of the school environment? During the pandemic, I asked my students whether they preferred the dark or light modes of the background of the shared screen. Most students said that the dark background is better. I prefer the dark as well. However, I do not think which one we choose in the classroom objectively matters. However, it matters that I asked.

It is good to remember that the preparation stage does not last only during class time or homework time. Students prepare their attention and knowledge during their entire life span, which is always ongoing. Thus, developing other stages has an impact on this stage. They think that I need this particular portion of the material soon or now, which certainly sharpens my attention. However, only really and sincerely wanting to know elevates my attention to the stars!

Exercise: In my classes, there are always several students who do not listen due to a variety of reasons. Some simply lack the skills to listen to English sufficiently well to pay attention for the entire hour. I have developed a brief experiment to find out who they are. After handing the students a piece of paper, I write instructions on the board and speak one instruction aloud, for example, to submit the paper on my desk before leaving the room. Then, I carefully observed the students and checked who submitted the paper after watching others doing it and who did not submit it at all. Some students had such a low attention span that they would take that paper. Sounds

*familiar? What are your methods related to observing students'
attention gaps?*

*Exercise: In your working environment (desk, office, home), identify
objects and features that help focus or generate distractions (visual,
sound, emotional, etc.). Remove and replace them with objects and
features that create calmness, focus, and attention. These
preferences may be very individual; thus, experiment with your
perception.*

Incubation

Imagine that during the preparation stage, students inquired about some
knowledge; now we visualize them walking home, engaging with other
chores, hoping that their subconscious will take care of all the heavy lifting
and integrate that new knowledge within their minds. However, this often
does not take place even in the slightest way. Students may return to class
the next day and claim that this portion of the material was not covered
since they do not have the slightest traces of it in their memory. So, what
triggers Incubation? Does it always happen? What are its circumstances?

As a high school student, I remember recalling all my classes from that
day during long walks on the beach. During those walks, I would frequently
solve math problems or "write" essays in my mind. Maybe the view of the
vast water or sand triggered those states of mind or a simple routine of a
"bored" mind that did those learning activities. As a young mathematics
student, I recall studying intensely on the bus, discussing math problems
at the bus stop, and keeping in mind all the unclear places of the lectures
so I could ask about them during office hours. I remembered a fellow
student confessing that he could only study at the central railway station
in Warsaw. Thus, studying for the linear algebra exam, he took all his
books and simply went to the station for a few days. Was it the feeling of
temporariness or being in motion, the station's charm, or simply waiting on

the bench (from now until an undefined future) without anything else to do? Anyways, he successfully prepared himself to solve challenging exam questions. I often reflect on those experiences, which makes me think that Incubation is not entirely subconscious. I believe it can be triggered by conscious encouragement of connections during the Preparation stage.

The entire trick for successful Incubation is to have a question in mind during Preparation. This is frequently overlooked in the teaching and learning process. We teach students some ready-to-serve content without inducing any questioning on their side. Without a clearly formulated question, the subconscious Incubation stage does not have any content to relate to. To encourage the Incubation stage, one can begin questioning during Preparation or create an intermediate stage for questioning. Here are some suggestions:

How is this new thing related to other things that I already know? If I combine this with another idea, what do they make together? What could I add to it? What kind of questions could I ask about it? Who invented this idea and why? How did they use it, and how did others use it? How would I use it? Can the idea be reformulated? Generalized? Or particularized? Can I explain it to a child or an elderly person using their language or examples? How would a child explain it to another child?

The Incubation stage may still not happen immediately but will wait until a habit of questioning is created over time. That is the feature of the subconscious mind, which may react instantly or after an extended period.

Exercise: What questions do you ask yourself while learning a new material?

Weisberg (Weisberg & Reeves, 2013) discusses possibly of forgetting during the Incubation stage of creative thought as initiated in (Woodworth, 1938). While some withdrawal from the problem and its temporary setup occurs, plain forgetting is doubtful. The researchers only tested participants encouraged to work on the problem again after a break. However, they did not study when and under what circumstances the solution of the problem occurs to people when they are not actually working at all and often are far away from their desks. They may be actively involved in other pursuits, such as driving, walking, eating, or shopping. This idea reminds me of a poet who writes poetry in the middle of the street, claiming that this place takes over the (conscious) attention and allows him to focus on deeper layers of subconsciousness. I am unsure whether I would like to read or study in a noisy room, but as a non-native English speaker, I can add that noise in English does not disturb me much and creates a form of soothing Humm.

I experimented with various light colors to understand their meaning to the mind (Cardoza & Marciniak, 2024). In my observations, the mind thought the room bathed in a red or violet light was simply a dream. In such a light, the mind disconnects from its habits, allowing new vibrations to emerge. I suspect the red color is associated with the sunset and imposes a state experienced right before sleeping.

Exercise: Make an experiment of studying in various environments to check what encourages the Incubation stage. You can try blue, green, red, or violet light. Try white noise, playing sports, taking walks, or anything else that comes to your mind. Check what can be accomplished with such an approach.

Illumination

The most mysterious and anticipated moment occurs when the idea from the subconscious arrives in the conscious mind. It may happen anytime and anywhere. This feeling may be beautiful and enlightening or painful. We should love it because it opens new doors and lifts us like angels. However, somehow, we fear it and avoid it. Well, nobody likes the sudden change of paradigms. Who among us liked the sudden turnaround during the pandemic? Who liked the return to "normal" afterward? Sudden illumination can break stereotypes and break the conveniently knitted semi-truths that are so cozy and pleasant.

Everybody experiences some illuminations daily, and it may be wise to oversee them and how they feel to the body and the mind. To experience illumination, the mind needs to be … well … empty and ready to receive a new thought. Constant social media scrolling, binge-movie watching, or this never-ending internal monologue will not be helpful. Alternatively, it actually may be; no one never knows for sure.

Multiple stories about fascinating, illuminating moments of famous scientists, writers, or artists exist. They often emphasize that this moment is involuntary, rare, and magical. While I entirely agree with Illumination's magical and mystical aspect, I will disagree with its rarity. I believe we can experience Illumination frequently during awake time, particularly right before falling asleep and right after waking up. There is a fine line between Illumination being involuntary but still somehow manageable. Illumination can be facilitated but cannot be controlled. We can influence it but not force it.

While preparing conference presentations, I frequently have to wait until the last minute to have the idea spark. This may be due to the urgent need to get it NOW and HERE without delays and further confusion. This stressful moment may entirely discourage some and motivate others. Try both. Which do you prefer? Which option does your mind prefer?

In the following exercise, observe how the mind can be convinced to work on some questions.

Exercise: Begin thinking of some questions before going to sleep. Then, set your alarm clock about 30 minutes before your usual time. Without moving your body too much or getting up, try to observe

24

what your mind is doing between the states of full awakening and complete sleep. Try to write down all the reasonable and nonsensical ideas that arrive without judging them. Just observe and take notes.

Illumination and religious enlightenment share certain features. Illumination resembles a "small" enlightenment.

Verification

The Verification stage may appear easy and enjoyable after experiencing the mysterious stages of Incubation and Illumination. However, it may carry certain discomforts, such as the possibility of being wrong and wasting effort, time, and energy. As a teacher, I very much dislike times when I make mistakes and need to admit them and correct them. I do not even want to think about the mess my mistakes made in my students' minds. However, is that so? The human mind and the human body are full of mistakes. Our DNA makes many mistakes when multiplying, but this does not prevent humankind from living longer than in previous centuries. Like DNA, human minds make multiple daily mistakes, some deadly and others insignificant. Recall that liability insurance was made precisely to ease the results of making mistakes. We no longer live in a society ruled by Hammurabi's codex with "Eye for eye and tooth for tooth." Thus, there is no need to make a big fuss about making a mistake while adding two fractions, especially when the results are not deadly. Moreover, many great discoveries were made "by mistake" or with specific "errors" but still led to extraordinary accomplishments. The continents of Americas were discovered during an attempt to go to India, penicillin was found in a filthy laboratory, and Coca Cola by a pharmacist who was trying a new recipe for painkillers. Admittedly, it takes some particular sensitivity to feel which ideas can produce valuable sprouts and separate them from those dull ideas.

While working with students or colleagues, I see this light in their faces when we arrive at good questions or answers. Even without consciously knowing what the discussion is about, I can immediately point out that there is some irrational excitement about this particular idea. I know that we will engage in the project with excitement, and by being engaged, we will stay active and tuned to the topic. Then, we will stay motivated while working on and completing the project.

However, while working alone, I used to loop around, not knowing which ideas were worthy of attention and which were not. Then I realized that the worthy ideas make me nearly tremble on the edge of discomfort, and I may not investigate them because of the intensity of the emotion. Nevertheless, with time, I began recognizing this feeling of a pounding heart and this energy. I learned to tame it and transform it into focus, motivation, and delight. Still, the beginnings were slow and laborious since I wanted to check every idea in detail.

Turbulent personalities may face challenges accepting their mistaken ideas as starters for further development. Assertive personalities may need to embrace the benefit of the doubt and pursue their "not knowing" paths while building verifications with each loop.

Whatever comes out of the mind during the Illumination stage must be meticulously analyzed (but not judged), thoughtfully considered, and verified. Displaying impatience or irritation will only ruin the vibes. However, how to hide your disappointment from yourself? Displaying judgment or disappointment is habitual behavior and can be modified with time and effort. At the same time, being overly lenient with new ideas will prevent them from further development. How to you find the right balance?

Repeating the loop

Simple things can be accomplished in one creative loop. However, most things around us reach a high level of complexity and need to be approached in multiple creative loops, making the discovery process a lengthy path. There is no other way. Thus, after the Verification stage, we find the gaps and the needs of the problem and try to fill in the blanks, returning to the Preparation stage.

I think that the first attempts at trying to experience creative stages may be somehow unsuccessful. In my understanding, this simply gives more room for trying. It may be wise to repeat the loop a few times with the same topic, and later, when this theme wears off, try something new.

Keeping a journal with notes from observations of one's mind may be laborious work but highly rewarding for anybody on any level of growth.

To start learning to be creative in STEM, one can begin with basic human activities related to dancing, movement, choreography, or sports. Cook something new, create a new recipe, or modify an existing recipe. You can try to compose new music or a song. Learn to paint or draw. Perform photography challenges, do arts and crafts, DIY projects, knitting, or sewing. Become a director of a short movie, which can be about your neighborhood or the library. While working on the book, I learned overtone singing (van Torgeren, 2023), which allows for the vast possibility of exploratory practices. Walking on a beach, I often sang to the clouds, the water, and the sand and made multiple attempts to find new sounds. Find a new group of people and do something you have never done before. At the same time when I was working on the book, I signed on to the webpage meetup.com and began attending sessions for group writing (via Zoom). Write, in particular, about your journey. Creating a journey is already a creative act.

Find a new teaching style and try to do one lesson in that style. Then, ask students for their suggestions. Was it valuable? Should it be expanded? Modified? Every semester, I ask my students for class structure and assignments suggestions. I asked along the way, but after the semester was over, I asked again for students' feedback, emphasizing that the lessons' topics and content were shaped over time with suggestions from many students.

After this introduction of the stages of creative thought and the idea of creative flow, the following revised definition of creativity can be formulated:

Creativity is a partly subconscious process of trials and reflections when something new to the student is made from something that is known or in the learning process.

Perceiving the Bull

I hear the song of the nightingale.
The sun is warm, the wind is mild,
Willows are green along the shore -
Here, no Ox can hide!
What artist can draw that massive head,
those majestic horns?

—3—

Creative Mathematics in the Light of Bloom's Taxonomy

History

The view of creativity from the perspective of the Bloom's Taxonomy went through a few transformations, and for further investigations, they will be briefly reviewed here. The first Bloom's Taxonomy (Bloom & Krathwohl, 1956) appeared in 1956 and contained several stages of learning but entirely ignored creative thinking. The improved Taxonomy from 1990 placed creativity on the top of the pyramid and shuffled the previous stages. The most recent Bloom's Taxonomy (from 2020) does not mention creativity separately but places it together in Extended Thinking with problem-posing and problem-solving. Comparison of these three taxonomies already appeared in literature and can be found, for example, in the paper by Anderson, et al (Anderson & Krathwohl, 2001).

Since the second Bloom's Taxonomy (the one from 1990) mentions creativity by name, it will be used here as a frame of reference that suits learning creative mathematics. At the end of the chapter, we will propose modifications to the pictorial representations of the stages that consider additional aspects discussed here.

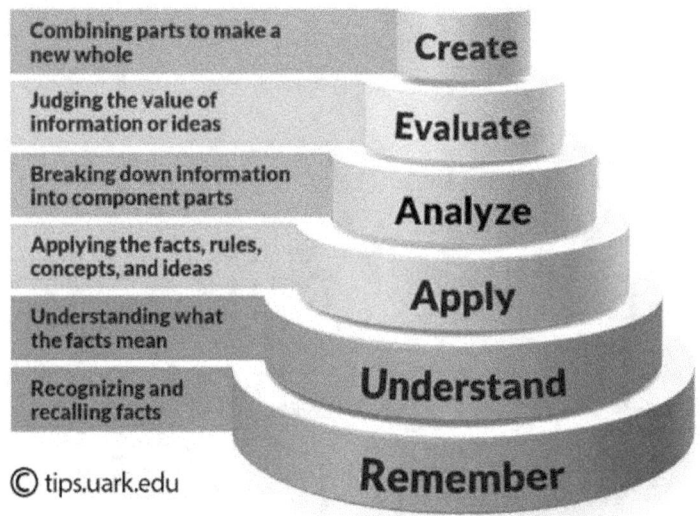

Figure. A classic picture of a Bloom taxonomy pyramid from
https://tips.uark.edu/using-blooms-taxonomy/

Basic View

The place of creativity in education was established in the 1990 Bloom's taxonomy at the very top of the pyramid, as seen in the figure above. The other five objectives of learning, placed below in the pyramid, are named as follows (from the bottom to the top): Remembering, Understanding,

Applying, Analyzing, and Evaluating. The placement of the objectives in the form of a pyramid suggests that the objectives of lower levels are necessary for performing the objectives of the higher levels. A mathematics teacher may doubt placing Remembering below Understanding since overemphasizing raw memorization in learning mathematics is a severe fault. We tend to explain mathematical ideas to allow them to be Remembered instead of Remembering them to be Understood. *I will use a sample method of teaching linear differential equations to give an example of those interactions. When introducing those equations, I will provide the definition and then explain some examples of linear differential equations.*

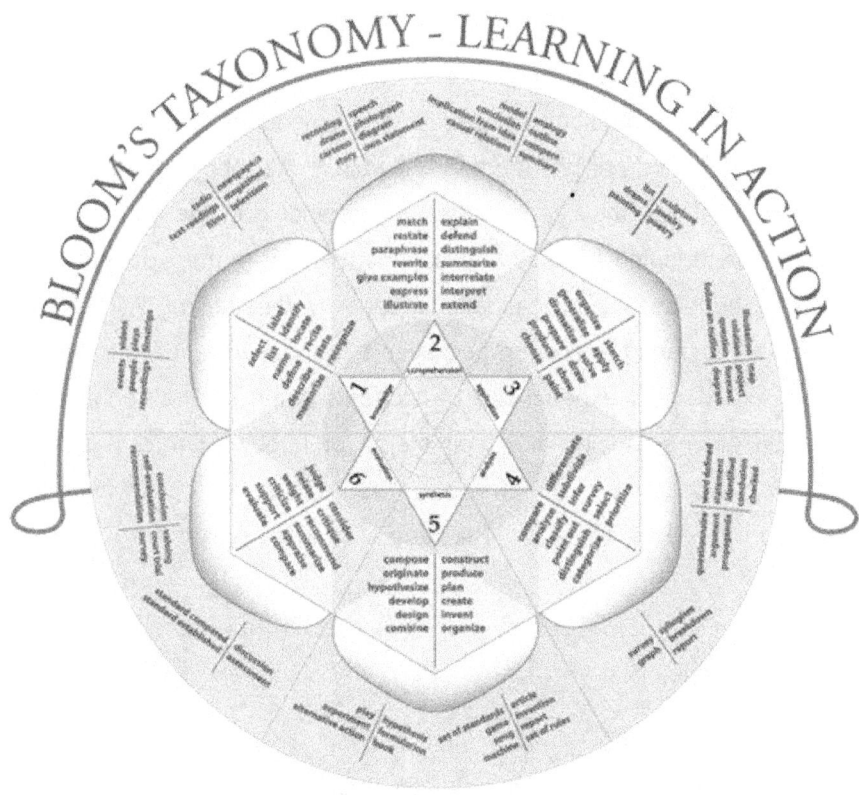

Figure. An Improved Taxonomy with a spiral inside indicating the circular aspect of learning from https://bloomstaxonomy.net/. This is still not entirely applicable to mathematics since the intuitive aspects of learning mathematics are omitted.

To display the interaction between those two objectives, Remembering and Understanding, one could explain that to Understand deeply and solely; students need to have the new material placed in short-term memory. Then, later, to place it in the long-term memory, they have to have it already understood. *Returning to the example about teaching linear differential equations, a lesson could continue with pointing out how the definition is aligned with the features of the sample equations. Providing counterexamples and highlighting how the definition is not aligned with their features may be educational.*

Similarly, when approaching Applications, often so demandingly requested by students in a math classroom, students need to have a particular understanding and primary memory. However, after applying the topic to specific situations, they get a better understanding of the nature of the topic. Thus, bringing to class Applications relevant to the students, their interests, hobbies, or significance encourages Understanding. At the same time, Remembering is encouraged even more due to repetition and the higher involvement experienced by students when seeing connections between the new topics and their major (or hobby). *The lesson can continue with some applications of linear differential equations. By this time of their studies, engineering students are probably already aware of the importance of Newton's law of heating and cooling. Seeing that a linear equation describes this law may be encouraging and motivating.*

Students can critically analyze their solutions or the solutions of their peers. They can attempt to Evaluate other students' work, possibly without assigning formal grades but with a percentage of completeness and correctness. Both Analyzing and Evaluating could be described as Reflecting, but unfortunately, this is not a part of the school curriculum. Math teachers often engage students in math classes in Analysis and Evaluation by providing historical and epistemological backgrounds for the topics. *Explaining the reasoning and meaning behind the terminology of the word "linear" in a broader context of equations of a single variable and multiple variables may not only give a better grip on the topic but also allow non-native speakers to expand their vocabulary.*

These objectives may be performed at the beginning of the lesson in the form of a game or a crossword. Similarly, basic Applications could serve as a motivation for building a more extensive theory and for introducing the topic. *In fact, the entire lesson about linear differential equations could begin with such a motivation.*

However, the pyramid does not visually represent these interactions of the five lower objectives of learning mathematics. Creativity in math classes seems even more problematic and challenging for teachers on all levels due to their lack of experience. Since math educators from most lower schooling levels rarely get involved in academic research, they lack such insight. Thus, they tend to neglect creative activities in the classroom, do not encourage them, and probably even discourage them, which is inappropriate for education. This generates a vicious circle of future teachers not being used to creative assignments and removing them from their classrooms.

Here is a simple creative activity that can accompany learning linear differential equations and incorporate multiple objectives from the Bloom's Taxonomy pyramid. After introducing the definition and a few examples, the instructor can ask students to provide their examples (this is Creative). Then, students can write their examples on the board to discuss them and justify which of them are indeed linear and which are not (this is Analyzing and Evaluating).

35

Recall that creative activities need to be facilitated by professionals with particular insight into creation who are fluent in various aspects of mathematics, not accompanied by fears and anxieties about the judgment of their performance.

The higher-level objectives solidify and cement the foundations since they engage multiple aspects of the mind, making humans perform complicated and aligning tasks. The higher levels in the hierarchy in the Taxonomy involve more complex and more rewarding activities; however, mastering the lower-level tasks is not mandatory for performing the higher-level tasks. Thus, using the traditional Pyramid to represent the Bloom's Taxonomy learning objectives may be misleading for mathematics instructors.

Relation to stages of creativity

The objectives of conscious learning from the Bloom's Taxonomy, called Remembering, Understanding, and Applying, resemble the conscious Preparation stage of the Wallas stages of creativity. The objectives of Analyzing and Evaluating may resemble the conscious stage of Verification. However, about Wallas stages of creativity, Bloom's taxonomy does not contain the subconscious stages of Incubation and the mysterious stage of Illumination. Another doubt about using the Bloom's Taxonomy for learning mathematics comes from a certain duality that features mathematics. It has (at least) two aspects, intuition, and formalism, and both are needed to perform, execute, or apply the topic to a broader scope. Thus, the Bloom's Taxonomy, entirely missing the intuitive aspect of learning mathematics, cannot address its issues adequately and is unsuitable as a frame of reference.

Detailed View

The Bloom's Taxonomy pyramid may appear relatively straightforward and natural, but anybody who has ever taught mathematics will look at it skeptically. Does the Bloom's Taxonomy apply to learning mathematics? Did any mathematicians have an influence when the descriptions were made? How should Taxonomy be modified to reflect on learning mathematics more accurately?

Here, I am recalling my students who can solve linear differential equations but display difficulties recognizing some of them among various examples.

However, the model does not reflect on that even if it claims reflections in the form of Analyzing and Evaluating. The linearity of the Bloom's Taxonomy makes it inflexible when specific math topics are likely to be taught by intuition first and then formalism. At the same time, others are in the opposite order. Thus, a new version should contain both conscious and subconscious aspects.

In this section, I will propose a generalized Bloom's Taxonomy that may suit mathematics instruction more precisely than the previous one. Moreover, the proposed generalization discusses mathematical formalism and intuition in the light of a circular nature of Learning (in the form of Remembering, Understanding, and Applying) and Reflections (in the form of Analyzing and Evaluating) connected by the moments of Creativity. Here is a proposition of a new taxonomy that emphasizes the circular nature of formal and intuitive learning with shifting moments of internalization and Creativity. Examples of the process of internalization in mathematics in the context of Creativity can be found in multiple works of William Baker, for example in (A Framework for Creative Insights Within Internalization, 2023).

0. Before introducing something new (to memorize), math teachers frequently discuss motivation and the need for such a thing. This way, they question and validate previous approaches, exposing their weaknesses and insufficiencies. While reflecting and debating on the insufficient aspects of the topic, they reveal moments of insight, sometimes with initial errors and wonders. Such an approach places the new topic among previously known topics. Often, applications may be helpful in placing this new topic in context. For example, while introducing graphs, one may take the problem of crossing Königsberg bridges and framing learning paths in terms of planar graphs and degrees of vertices.

1. After an epistemological or historical introduction, we provide an intuitive description and (or) a formal definition of the new topic. Students may be able to partially repeat that definition depending on its complexity, but most mathematical topics are relatively resistant to blind memorization.

2. Depending on the topic's complexity, one can attempt to ask students to provide some examples and reflect whether provided samples are indeed examples or not, and what prevents them from being examples. After such an exercise, students should be able to recognize the new object among other similar objects or identify obstacles. This activity certainly helps students memorize the objects by placing them among others, similar but not the same. To provide an example, I would bring up the topic of linear equations, where students need to write down their examples and justify them one way or another after seeing a few examples of such equations. This helps with relatively shallow Understanding. Similarly, after seeing a procedure, students should be able to follow it in an analogical situation (but not likely with an entirely different situation).

Frequently, class meetings finish at this point of learning trajectory, and the teacher giving a quiz on that topic may be amazed that an impressively responding group of students does not remember much within a week of the class. Thus, by giving a quiz next week,

38

the teacher finds out that grades are low, and anxiety among the students is high. This may serve as a motivation for more elaborate lectures, more applications, student projects, and additional quizzes since the feedback loop is a crucial part of learning.

3. After solving a few new topic examples, students may be ready to apply the learned material. In the first round, students would apply the learned math topic in textbook problems, following the footprints of previous examples. They may also attempt to find the parameters of a model with given data. However, all of these assignments and skills are within known paths. There are some additional challenges carried by applications. As much as mathematics may be frustrating, applications are a true conceptual maze for many students.

While teaching Calculus 3 to engineering students, I often heard requests for applications, but at the same time, students asked to remove them from the tests. At first, I found this behavior somewhat confusing. However, after speaking with students, I discovered that not all engineering students know the same applications. For example, civil and mechanical engineering programs do not teach circuits (that topic may be discussed while introducing ordinary differential equations). However, at the same time, electrical engineering students may not be very excited about pendulum equations. While all of them may be curious about linear algebra applications in image processing, they do not feel comfortable enough with the background material to be tested on math in that context.

4. Unfortunately, most learning objectives of the modern curriculum stop at this point without making further steps up on the pyramid. The challenge of the next step is to attempt to internalize the topics learned before. Unfortunately, it is not a part of the curriculum to mingle with the students' minds and perceptions. However, the truth is that successful learning must

gain an insight into how the mind works and what it takes to internalize learned topics to the point where learners consider the ideas their own and a part of their mind's routines of thought. The critical point here is the spontaneous shifting from conscious external learning to subconscious internal learning.

5. The internal aspects of learning begin with conscious reflections in the form of analysis and questioning of the learned concepts. For some people, this may happen right after they see the concept for the first time. Internalization may be considered a sign of mature learning. Often, this may be triggered in teachers by insightful students who ask inquisitive questions and motivate the teacher to perform more profound reflections about the topic. An essential aspect of analyzing may be when students find new properties of previously learned structures or observe similarities and differences among the structures on their own. Students' progress in this aspect may be observed when they tutor or teach one another or provide feedback for someone's work or textbook quality. This stage may be motivated by regular textbook homework assignments assisted by additional questions where students need to reflect on the answer and provide some insight. In my experience, students often ignore non-mathematical and non-scholarly questions unless they are encouraged to respond in clear and explicit ways.

6. Debate may be an excellent way for professionals to internalize mathematics, but students frequently report that they do not want to say something stupid to appear silly. That is why they prefer to say nothing than to say too much. Thus, this form of evaluating mathematical concepts may be, in some instances, a questionable way of internalization but very efficient in others.

7. The culminating point of internal processes (of Wallas' Incubation) can be the AHA! Moment of creative insight that may appear suddenly to a knowledgeable and reflecting mind. However, since creativity often

40

appears in surprising moments, such as the middle of the night, one still needs to remember the vision-like appearance of the solution (which closes the loop, sending us to the beginning of the learning process). The first appearance of creative ideas may be blurry and unclear; they still require work, understanding, and application attempts before they are analyzed and evaluated, leading to ground-breaking discoveries.

The ideas described above are represented in the picture below. The subconscious is represented as the space (water and air) where the learning objectives occur. The Inquiry is represented by the person (the meditating mind) in the center of the picture since it decides how to place new topics in a context. New information does not find its place among other topics without proper context. The other objectives are organized according to their simplicity: Remembering is a swimmer; it represents the fact of plain motion. The simple yacht represents Understanding and is more sophisticated than the swimmer but less sophisticated than the large sailboat, representing Analysis. Evaluation is displayed as a motorboat and Application as an airplane. I hope that the airplane gives the idea that the actual applications may be very advanced, sometimes more advanced than the topic itself and way beyond the existing comprehension of the students. Creativity is displayed as a submarine to emphasize the subconscious aspect of it since the submarine spends most of its time under the water. There are no arrows to show the direction of growth since the pictures are already placed on the circle. Moving from one picture to the other, the mind has to go through the water to indicate that internalization and subconscious learning must occur. Just like being able to sail or operate a motorboat or an airplane does not imply mastery of the swimming skill, the learning objectives are somehow independent in the big picture.

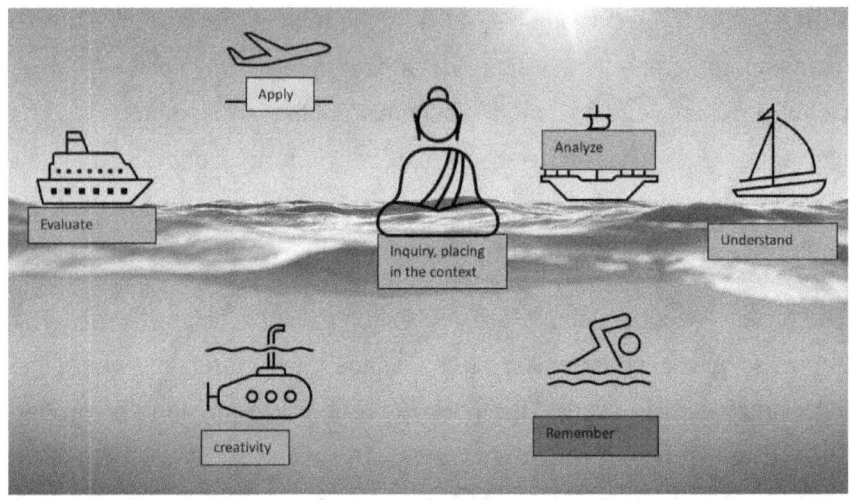

Figure. My artistic vision of the Bloom Taxonomy.

Further ideas

This analysis of the Bloom's Taxonomy is somewhat incomplete and will be developed further in light of the projects presented in the next part of the book. It will become clear that the learning process appears in cyclic rounds, starting with an inquiry or a need. Then, it goes through external and internal aspects. The Bloom's taxonomy recognizes the moment of shifting from internal to external learning as Creativity. However, it remains silent about spontaneous shifting from external learning (in the form of Remembering, Understanding, and Applying) to internal learning (in the form of Analyzing and Evaluating). Indeed, a skillful and aware teacher can facilitate such a shift. However, without making this habit of internalization, most teaching and learning efforts may be entirely wasted for generations.

Here, I attempted to be creative and pictorially represent the Bloom's taxonomy as I see it in my imagination. However, this can be done in many ways. I would encourage the readers to create their pictorial representations of Taxonomy to encourage communicating with imagination.

Math anxiety? Test anxiety?

Unfortunately, most college curricula do not go beyond mathematics Applications, often overemphasizing the objectives of Remembering. This curriculum structure is the reason for multiple complaints from students who claim they knew and understood the material at home but somehow forgot everything during the test. Similarly, students say they know how to solve a problem at home, but when they come to school, they forget how the solution should be implemented. This lack of consistency in retrieving the knowledge or the skills results from the objectives being fulfilled lightly and not being solidified by higher-level activities.

Teachers on all levels realize that their students do not retain the material from class to class and forget easily. To address this issue, the material is then repeated over and over without much success creating further frustration among the teachers and students. The lack of creative activities in the math classroom results in math anxiety among students, which, over time, builds into a genuine reluctance and even disgust. Accompanied by exorbitant expectations and consistently low performance, this feeling may transform into math and testing anxiety disorders. Amazingly, students, when engaged in exciting activities (such as applications, discussions, analysis, evaluation, or creative assignments), do not have difficulties with memory, focus, and understanding. However, these exciting activities that involve creative applications, analysis, and evaluation of one's work or the work of others are pushed away from the mainstream to give more space for Remembering.

Forget Basic Skills Courses

Courses that aim to improve students' basic skills are genuinely a big pedagogical mistake in education since their only goal is remembering. But even Understanding of basic topics cannot be fulfilled by listening to lectures and performing basic calculations. Without performing higher objectives of the Bloom's taxonomy, students will remain in the stages of weak memorization and even weaker understanding (Parker, Traver, & Cornick, 2017). As mentioned before, students often demand applications of mathematical concepts, but at the same time, they request that these applications do not appear on the test. As this may sound contradictory, it is entirely justified by the fact that students need to engage in objectives higher in the Bloom's taxonomy to be comfortably tested on the objectives placed lower.

If taught for kids, basic skills math courses may involve "silly" creativity when kids play for example with shapes or colors that represent numbers. However, adults or teens will not be satisfied with this type of creativity and will be unable to engage in more sophisticated types of creativity without judgment, preventing their success in basic skills courses. The differences between child and adult creativity are the theme for the next chapter.

Catching the Bull

I seize him with a terrific struggle.
His great will and power
are inexhaustible.
He charges to the high plateau
far above the cloud-mists,
Or in an impenetrable ravine he stands.

—4—

Child vs. Adult Creativity

The title of this chapter may appear to be stated very lightly, but it is, in fact, a topic for another book or even a few books. It is in the reader's interest to start the creative journey at the early stages of the development of the human mind to recall the creative vibes of a child. Sadly, there is no coming back to that stage and those feelings. However, the memories may serve as a frame of reference for further considerations of creativity being a natural function of human minds.

In the theory of Piaget (McCarthy Gallager & Reid, 2002) (pages 221, 229) a child is born with creativity and can lose it while trying to fit into society's values and norms. However, Vygotsky (Frawley, 1997) sees it somehow in an opposite light, saying, "In the process of historical development, social man changes the methods and devices of his behavior... and develops and creates new forms of behavior- specifically cultural".

Assuming that the readers are either teachers or students at the high school or academic level, I will not elaborate on the role of creativity in children's development but focus on the ways of losing it in the process of growth and education.

It may be surprising, but as an adult, I still remember those times when, as a child, I would sit down and play. I could do it for hours in silence and be busy with myself. My endless imagination told me fabulous stories, played sounds, or showed images that could not be created by anybody else. Indeed, I did not know how to name the state of mind that I was experiencing. I only knew that it was delightful and satisfying. As kids, we are incredibly creative but without intellectual reflection on the results of that creation. I did not revise my stories; I did not tell them again; they were fresh and new every time they reached me.

Exploratory nature of children's minds

Observing infants does not leave any doubts and brings immediate conclusions that children left alone begin spontaneous explorations of their possibilities. Such explorations may be related to one's own body or immediate surroundings. They may include touching and feeling the knuckles, feet, knees, or some objects with the tongue or hands. Once kids begin to lift their heads, they will try to look around, and once they can sit, they will try to stand up or walk on four limbs. As soon as they stand, they will attempt to take a step. They will walk around and later run around. This is a natural process of exploring one's capacity for movement. Shall this be considered creative? Since children observe others moving around, sitting, or walking, it is difficult to claim that what they do is entirely creative. However, they are within their minds searching for new options among things already observed. Interestingly, similar exploratory processes happen in relation to the mental stream. Once a child observes the mental processes of others, they will explore them, mimic them, and learn about their places and structures. It is not a mystery that babies open their mouths wide when seeing someone smiling or may make a long face when seeing someone sad. Then, when on their own or in a company, they will explore recently observed mental streams and study them according to their perception.

These explorations of body and mind are natural and involuntary. However, without them, children would not have a chance to grow their psycho-motoric skills to match the requirements of modern society. Reflecting on this "creativity" of a child, we often fail to realize that children are merely searching within the frames of the surrounding reality but usually do not cross its boundaries. If creativity describes a process of developing something new, children fail to be creative if they rely only on imitation or repetition. To the parents, the actual level of the creative skill of their child may remain hidden if they do not know what the child was exposed to in kindergarten, on TV or, literally, through a keyhole.

The situation changes rapidly for a teenager who, in creating their alignment from a scattered patchwork of spontaneously accepted truths or semi-truths, sometimes needs to break inconsistent stereotypes represented by different reality frames incepted by various sources. The main difficulties lay in creating space for agreements among different frames, which cut the reality across different planes. This process is a form of self-calibration or self-learning of a neural network where the network creates its own identity and becomes aware of it. Thus, the true creativity of the mind begins within self-creation in sometimes violent processes of strengthening and quieting previously learned neural circuits.

As the knowledge of the internal and external reality develops, the growing individual naturally engages less in explorations and gradually begins to engage more in using the established knowledge. This is entirely understandable since the sense of knowing carries the feeling of certain comfort and balance and the sense of not knowing may be associated with feeling lost and helpless. However, the vulnerable sense of not knowing may motivate explorations of the boundaries of own capacity. This may be expressed in a way of searching for new continents, starting a scientific revolution, or developing impressionism. Both attitudes, relying on knowledge and restless explorations, have benefits and drawbacks.

The comfort of knowing may be more efficient than the virtuous inquiry of not knowing because it simply uses less mental energy, as visualized by the following example. Imagine someone searching for an excellent way to walk to a nearby shopping mall. At first, the path is new and energy-consuming, but after a few trips, it becomes more predictable and requires less attention. The energy preserved during that process can be applied to something else, such as searching for an improved path or exploring things along the known path. Subconscious energy calculations shape the mind's preferences for explorations or known things. Always saying that you do not want to explore new paths since the one you know is good enough may be an efficient (but boring) way to live.

It may seem that a child's period of exploration and creativity diminishes significantly after puberty. However, life has its ups and downs, and as adults, we frequently go through challenging situations that flip our world around. They may make us feel miserable but are, in fact, the reasons and fuels for creativity and transformation. The mature mind quickly realizes its lack of preparation for personal crises and begins its journey of realization. I understand that blaming education for shrinking students' exploratory nature and creative mindset is an overstatement. Think about the times 200 years ago when students did not receive any schooling. Was the world full of exceptionally creative people? Or it was full of unenlightened individuals who lived in darkness?

However, saying that education could motivate us to explore more is undoubtedly true.

Discouragements

A child neglects creative vibes due to multiple reasons, which may be external or internal. It would be expected that the most dedicated introverts will lean more toward internal reasons, while the most dedicated extroverts will lean toward external reasons. However, since an average human is, in one way or another, a dedicated ambivert, combining both introverted and extroverted features, it is the most reasonable to assume that both reasons apply to both personality features.

Some external reasons for abandoning creative vibes may lie along the following paths: the teachers, parents, siblings, and peers display reactions toward creative processes or creations.

- Intuitive: Bad face, disgust, unspoken disapproval, just a simple lack of interest while showing a sincere interest in unoriginal works.

- Sensing: Bad grade or penalty received for a creative approach that does not "fit in the box."

- Intentional or unintentional pressures to modify or alter the creative process or its results.

- Being judged for appearing weird during the creative process, having dreamy eyes, being spaced out, not listening to others, not paying attention, and missing directions or guidelines.

- Being rewarded for following the guidelines to the point and being discouraged from thinking individually.

- Being discouraged from working on original projects (painting, for example) while being encouraged to spend time on repetitive projects (solving tavern puzzles, for example).

Some internal reasons for abandoning creative vibes may lie along the paths where a child or an adolescent experience repeatedly self-discouragement or lacks encouragement in the following ways:

- Self-judgement expressed as a disapproval of the creative process results, seeing the results as unappealing and unsatisfactory.
- Feeling the creative process as painful, unusual, creepy, or wild. Experiencing the Preparation stage as lengthy or tedious. Experiencing the Incubation stage as uncontrollable or not knowing whether it even happens. Experiencing the Illumination stage as scary or inappropriate. Experiencing the Verification stage as inadequate or overly critical.
- Feeling discomfort while awaiting the judgment of others, being afraid of criticism, not being able to accept even the slightest criticism or dispute of own work.
- Not seeing a value in the creative process or its results.
- In the long run, not feeling sufficient joyous thrill from the process and not sufficiently satisfied with the results.
- Consistently reaching the known instead of the unknown out of convenience or mental coziness.
- Benefiting more from being non-creative and enjoying those benefits.
- In addition, creative processes may require specific lone time, which may be uncomfortable for extroverts. Defending one's creation may require group time, which introverts may find uncomfortable.

The lists above are not exhaustive but may ring some bells and explain why your creative vibes shrink over time. Recalling it may be easier if they relate to one situation involving criticism or one memorable event. However, this could be mild and unrelated to any memorable time, making the shift less detectable. Like cumulative trauma, this cumulative discouragement of creativity may be more impactful and challenging to undo than one unpleasant but well-remembered event. Keeping this in mind, we begin discussing the features of creativity of a mature mind.

While giving a toddler a toy, we may expect to find it in a toilet bowl because the child wants to check whether it would fit in the opening. This is already sufficiently satisfying for a child to accommodate the creative impulse. An adolescent or an adult would not do that because this kind of creativity is not attractive to them and does not carry any exciting questions or results. As adolescents or mature people, we have more informed tastes in what we find satisfying. However, at the same time, we may fear judgment or be easily discouraged by the displeasing results of our creation. Thus, adults may find certain creative activities impractical or wasteful regarding time, effort, or energy. However, they may find other creative activities helpful, beautiful, and engaging.

Creativity of a mature mind

While teaching at a college, one quickly realizes that adolescent students may be sharp and witty, but mature students tend to be more preceptive and successful. They are more motivated, apply themselves more accurately, and make more connections among the topics. They are also more tempted to ask questions, engage in conversations with the teacher, and are more responding to teacher requests. As much as these signs of involvement are not signs of creativity, they are signs of transformation. Mature students who return to school report frequently not caring much about school and learning in their youth. While listening to their life stories, I realized that they all underwent certain transformations that changed their attitudes toward learning. In my understanding, they went through moments of spontaneous or forced creative insights related to the importance of their states of mind for their success. Surprisingly, when reading about Rober Kegan's (Kegan, 1982) Constructive-Developmental

Theory of the growth of the mindset of adults, I found multiple points of alignment with the idea of consciously (re-)developing the skill of creativity.

Kegan's theory

As a teacher, I understand that my mind and the minds of my colleagues go through multiple transformations and re-validations imposed by never-ending professional development, excessive reading, insightful reflections, deep discussions, being on display in a classroom, being willing to provide quality instruction, and demanding external and internal environments. However, at the same time, I understand that this may not be the case for all adults, especially those who are not forced by the circumstances of life or work to keep developing themselves. Kegan (Kegan, 1982) defined five (or six, depending on the year of his work) orders of thinking, where each is more complex than the previous one. They are called developmental orders of mind and are related to how the mind creates a sense of its own experiences.

Kegan's theory analyzes the evolution of consciousness from a basic perspective to a significantly developed perspective. For the sake of completeness of the exposition, the orders are presented here in the context of creativity (after Kegan's "Forms of Mind" 2000)

Order 0. The mind of a newborn is up to 18 months when the concept of an object is not defined yet.

Order 1. The Impulsive Mind is a feature of young children (up to 6 years old) where impulses (for example, curiosity) are the main driving force of their minds. In this order, children do not display awareness of their creative forces. Creativity cannot be temporarily suppressed or called. It cannot be analyzed or reflected upon.

Order 2. The Instrumental Mind causes a child (from 6 years old to adolescence) to live according to their needs and wishes. Creativity can be suspended temporarily or called as needed when it contributes to the needs of the self. Surprisingly, early adolescents can display their vision of themselves, often being very creative. I recall many of my colleagues and myself at that age writing poetry and prose, composing music, sewing my own clothes, or having many ideas entirely "out of the box." However, verifying those ideas and receiving constructive feedback was not easy. Thus, the reflections on the results of creative vibes may be challenging, and the reflections on the creative process are not frequent or natural in this order of mind.

Order 3. The Socialized Mind may be responsible for shifting from spontaneous creativity to other activities encouraged more by society or by one's imagination of the societal expectations. The sense of self is based on fitting in the group and characterizes post-adolescence. This may be the order when creativity is abandoned to some extent due to the fear of being judged. However, circumstances and individual needs may override the general preferences of this stage. Students in this order accept the axioms of arithmetic straight from the book of Aristotle and follow to the point if that is socially expected.

Order 4. Self-Authoring Mind does not need societal validation to create a set of values for themselves. Self-identity is created based on values, ideology, and vision of one's progress. This process requires multiple creative cycles and an accurate, concise, consistent creative flows. Thus, it takes time and consistent effort to complete this order successfully. In this order, the axioms of arithmetic are reformulated and revised according to one's vision. They are compared to the classic axioms but held in a separate compartment.

Order 5. A Self-Transforming mind is on the path of creating one's visions of growth and direction and revalidating and reformulating this vision as needed. Such a mind can discuss one's elaborate ideologies, compare them to others, and reflect on them. In particular, a mind of this order can encourage or discourage certain vibes, such as creativity. This order sees the classic axioms and many other versions of axioms aligned or misaligned and freely compares their realities without judgments.

Students from each order display a different style of their narrative and different attitudes toward learning, in particular, learning creativity. In most of my classes, most students have a Socialized Mind and are very sensitive to the opinions of others. More details on this topic and students' narratives can be found in the study by Eleanor Drago-Severson about transformational learning of adults (Drago-Severson, 2004).

It is worthwhile to mention that being able to perform in the frame of one developmental order skillfully does not prevent one from being able to perform, when suitable, on other, lower orders; attempting to perform on a particular order does not mean that this attempt is always successful and does not mean that this order is mastered. Interestingly, having the intention for one's growth belongs to order 4 (Self-Authoring Mind). While taking the responsibility to develop creativity in oneself belongs to the 5th, the highest development order (Self-Transforming Mind). This may be a good point to reflect on the natural continuation of the theory into further orders. What would be the following order for an ever-developing mind? In my understanding, a natural continuation of the theory would be the willingness to contribute to the self-transformations of other minds, but this may already touch the enlightened minds' magic. Thus, it will not be discussed in depth here, leaving the topic for further consideration by the readers.

While reflecting on the theories and the timeline of Kegan's discovery, I realized that the previous generations might not have observed the patterns of the adults growth. This oversight likely occurred because the average human lifespan was not long enough to recognize these patterns as a population-wide phenomenon rather than traits of specific individuals. I only wonder what future discoveries will bring when, generation by generation, we experience changes not seen before. Human beings are certainly still a subject of evolution, but while bodies may not undergo visible transformations, minds may undergo measurable transformations with refined measuring tools.

I hope tapping into creativity throughout Order 3 may increase the chances of (ever) entering Orders 4 and 5. While this statement may become statistically significant after a few generations of readers, I decided to take a calculated risk and direct this exposition to teachers and students.

The takeaway from Kegan's theory is that students in math classes may be on various orders of mind and may display entirely different attitudes toward the class, teachers, other students, and creative assignments. Thus, the results of such assignments are expected to be on a particular spectrum. Usually, in my college classes, at least one student does not do well in the creative aspects of the class project. However, at the same time, there is usually this one student whose project is extraordinary in creativity.

Reflections

It seems that a minority of the population. (Kegan, 1982) reaches the last order of development, and the others simply remain within the scope of the previous orders. Thinking about the reasons for growth, one can reflect on the lack of growth in the following way: for growth, it is necessary to experience suitable challenges that are possible to tackle. An average person experiences numerous challenges on various levels, but the questioning of reality may be insufficient for creating new solutions. Again, this is a problem of personal creativity. However, to defend those not growing to the highest levels, one can mention that children's levels are enhanced and encouraged by multiple interactions with those who have already mastered those higher levels (older siblings, other older children, adults, etc.). However, the growth to the highest orders is not always assisted by such interactions since rare examples from those in the minority may not be broadly available. One may argue that literature is full of such examples, but literature is not the same as life experience; using such examples as a base for generalizations requires a certain leap of growth.

Looking back at the stages of development of a child and a student, one could ask, where and how should the journey to creative education begin? Creative education should begin as early as possible in the best version and continue through all stages. However, as of today, seeing that creativity is lost somewhere on the path to college, where should the transformation begin? In the minds of the teachers? Or in the minds of the students? Preferably both simultaneously. Since the students will grow their minds based on the observations of the minds of their teachers, the place to begin the creative leap is professional development for teachers. However, with the resistance of the students' creativity, it will not bloom in the classroom.

I believe that tapping into teachers' exploratory nature and their need for creativity can spark the motivation for the growth of creative thoughts among students in the future.

Taming the Bull

The whip and rope are necessary,
Else, he might stray off down.
some dusty road.
Being well-trained, he becomes
naturally gentle.
Then, unfettered, he obeys his master.

—5—

Self-Development

Warmup

The development of one's creativity is a starting point for developing awareness of creativity to facilitate it in the classroom. It is essential to realize that encouraging others to be creative does not exclude teachers without fully developed skills. It is available to teachers whose creativity is still a "work in progress." Moreover, encouraging others may be a way to strengthen self-motivation and pursue creativity skills further and more substantially, whatever that means. In the last chapter of the book, "Creativity, the psychology of Discovery and Invention," Csikszentmihalyi (1996) devotes themself to personal creativity. That is where this chapter begins.

The path of developing one's creativity, as understood as restructuring one's vision of self, is neither smooth nor straightforward. Robert Kegan describes it in "The Evolving Self" (Kegan, 1982) on page 215:

"All growth is costly. It involves the leaving behind of an old way of being in the world. Often it involves, at least for a time, leaving behind the others who have been identified with that old way of being..."

However, it must be this way. While the benefits of being creative are undeniable, there is one significant drawback: you must abandon your former self. You must bid farewell, as you will never be the same again.

However, maybe before we begin a journey of (re)creating your creativity, it is worthwhile to briefly examine the possibility that you are already creative in some way but do not see or do not value it. Are you being creative, maybe even every day, with small things that go unnoticed? Or possibly with your work. As an educator designing lessons and activities for your students, you may engage in creative processes daily without even recognizing it as significant. *Create a list of activities, accomplishments, and practicalities that you perform, which may involve some creative thinking.* Here is a list of various activities that may involve creativity:

- in visual arts,
- in performing arts, singing, playing, dancing, acting,
- poetry, writing,
- in science and technology, formal sciences,
- computer science, creating new apps,
- in engineering, finding new applications, solving practical problems,
- creating own recipes while cooking or baking.

Get ready with a pen and a piece of paper to get a record of your progress.

Exercise. Here is a simple exercise for self-assessment of your creativity. Get an ordinary object that you can find around yourself. What is its purpose? Now, think about six ways you used or could use this object that does not align with its original purpose. Take a pencil, for example. Did you use it as a bookmark? Did you use it to put your hair up? For leveling the projector? Within a few-minute brainstorming session, write down six examples of applications of this object that are not its original purpose, analyze the results, and have a quick look at the ideas and their shapes.

To observe changes in creative thinking, one needs to be able to apply specific measures. While stereotypic thinking considers only social appreciation of the final results of the creative process, more insightful measures suitable for educational purposes consider various factors. Some measures are subjective, like the easiness of arriving at thoughts, and others are objective (but still self-observed), such as the number of unusual applications written down within a few minutes.

Exercise. Now, observe the shape of your thinking. Do various ideas arrive in the mind naturally and smoothly? Or does thinking outside of the box come with difficulties?

There are many ways to observe the improvement of one's own progress informally. How many examples were you able to provide within the first minute? Did they all jump at you at once, or were they coming successively? What kind of mind frame did you have when they were coming? Can you provide the chain of associations that led you to each example? How diverse are the examples? Did you provide six ways of holding up your hair with a pencil? Or the applications are diverse? What aspects of the object did you use? The shape, color, transparency? Smoothness or sharpness? Do all of your examples use one aspect or a variety of them? Did you only use the fact that a pencil is a long, slim object? Or do your examples incorporate other aspects of that pencil? How surprising and unusual are the examples that you mentioned?

Exercise. While thinking about how to order the chapters in a logical flow, I recalled that according to the theory of relativity, time is an illusion; thus, the time of our lives is also an illusion. The life we perceive in chronological order does not have a linear structure but happens "simultaneously." Amazingly, we do not have a dilemma displaying our adolescence after our teenage years and both after childhood. Now, let us think about the impossible and imagine that something broke in the mind and randomly displays the days of someone's life. Days of being an elderly person may be followed by days as a toddler. How would you live your life in such circumstances? How would this change you and your attitudes?

This exercise includes a hint of other exercises that can be invented "on the go". Simply choose one feature of reality and alter it to your liking. Then elaborate on the implications of that change. *Exercise. Since the concept of the observer appears in philosophy and physics, I like to reflect on it frequently. Observation (observer effect) or performing measurements (uncertainty principle) is known to change the results of the entire experiment or affect other measurements. Due to human nature, this is observable in the space of human behaviors. Have you seen it? Can you mention another physics phenomenon or mathematical structure observable in human behaviors or interactions?*

The good news is that no matter what measurements are taken into consideration, reflecting on creative thought and starting the process of development of thoughts improves all of them. More importantly, it improves self-awareness and self-satisfaction.

Exercise. We can find something impossible by altering one factor of a known thing. Choose an object around, an idea, or a natural phenomenon and alter one property to obtain the impossible. Imagine a house where the windows open only from the outside. I got this nonsense idea because my desk was near the window, and I was looking at the handle, imagining it on the other side. Indeed, get into a habit of being able to track your thoughts to know what inspired you.

To practice and encourage creativity, invent something impossible and … enjoy the process. This could be, for example, a game or a … mind exercise. Every day, I will create a fun mind exercise, play with it, and observe how it changes my thinking. Every time, I will lay down the circumstances of how the idea arrived, giving the motivation for the exercise, hoping that the readers will be able to compose their exercises responding to their needs.

Something impossible may appear to the mind while using analogies with known things and posing generalizing questions. Sometimes inspiration comes while doing something with one's own hands, but sometimes it may come during visualizations. The most precious moments are when, after developing some insight, the impossible proves to be possible. Imagine how the ancient people drew circles using a string of the same length as the desired radius. Imagine that instead of a stick to hold the string at the center of the circle, you would use a cylinder wrapped around the string. If you are a mathematician, you may develop the formula for the spiral obtained by unwrapping (or wrapping) the string. Non-mathematicians are encouraged to create their own exercises suitable for their interest, education, and comprehension.

Exercise. Here is the parametrization of such a spiral. Assuming that the cylinder has a radius a and the initial distance from the string to the cylinder is b then the spiral can be described in terms of polar *coordinates as $r(t) = a(t + 1) + b$, where t is the angle and r is the radius. In terms of a parametrization that gives:*

$$\vec{r}(t) = \langle (a(t + 1) + b) \cos t, (a(t + 1) + b)\sin t \rangle$$

However, this thought can go further and grow in multiple directions, you decide for example:

- *instead of a cylinder, one could use another shape. What kind of shape would you use, and how would it affect the shape of the spiral?*
- *Imagine that the string is sliding slightly on the surface of the cylinder. How does this affect the spiral?*
- *mathematically, we can assume that the string's thickness is irrelevant to its position, but adding some thickness to it would make the radius of the cylinder change as the string is being unwrapped from it. This feature would add another parameter to the model. How would the shape of the spiral change?*
- *instead of thinking in 2 dimensions, one could try to see this situation in 3 dimensions. Could a sphere be drawn that way? What shapes and their formulas can be obtained by altering the center into another closed surface?*
- *make your own direction along with your ideas close to your heart. What are they? Where are they coming from?*

Recall that the attitude of a baby when she gets a new toy is "What can I do with it?" while a mature person (with Kegan's Socialized Mind) asks, "What is this for?". The differences between a baby and a mature mind may lie in experience. Children have minimal experience and need to try things before they settle with some "knowledge." We often think we already know enough, which closes the door to free trying. Alternatively, our creativity may be clogged by trusting authority too much. This section served as a warmup for returning to this original vibe, which later needs to be expanded by the further and more elaborate stages of creative thought, such as preparation and verification, and later leads to the creative flow.

Daily Experience of Creativity

We are taught to admire the outstanding accomplishments and creativity of others, unfortunately often omitting the long process it took to arrive at the result. This leads to a misconception that creativity is reserved for the gifted and the learned to make significant scientific discoveries or great art that finds its place at a museum. However, the truth is somehow on the other end of the spectrum. According to Koestler's bisociation (Koestler, 1964) the frequent and daily use of powerful creative flow liberates the mind from overwhelming habits.

As mentioned, most people (Kegan, 1982) experience most of their creativity during their childhood. However, the results of this creativity may not have many applications, nor are they reflected upon. Being college professors, we could claim that we are creative daily while finding new research topics or working on research projects. However, it does not mean that only highly educated individuals can be creative validly and with valuable topics. We can be creative daily with daily chores and mundane activities regardless of our education and employment. Moreover, this can be a source of immense joy. Recently, I received some guidelines for making sushi. The idea of repeating the same procedure without adding anything new seemed quite unbearable to me. However, searching for new ingredients and testing them in sushi felt quite appealing. After placing colorful ingredients on the wrap and cutting the roll into pieces, I realized that the distribution of the shapes and colors in the resulting cuts is unpredictable, encouraging numerous experiments. At the same time, a friend of mine created mini sushi. The joy of creating artistically appealing shapes and colors in a small bite of food was quite immense. Then, reflecting on how placing ingredients on the rice affects the look and the taste of pieces of sushi after rolling and cutting was quite an entertaining activity.

While rediscovering the skill of creativity, the mature mind treats it as a novelty and studies it in various versions, particularly in casual situations (Koestler, 1964). This allows the skill to grow, and eventually, the mind becomes fluent in creativity. Particular thrills and excitements that assist creative flow make creativity even more attractive to the mind. As my students pointed out in their conference proceedings presentation (Torres, 2018).

'Creativity is not something that I do during the project. I do it every day and all the time.'

Everyday creativity allows us to deal with multiple daily struggles successfully: fix a leaning shelf with remainders from a broken hook or find out how to overcome problems with equipment that is not working correctly. At the same time, allowing creativity daily makes the creative skill truly functional and available when needed for challenging research questions.

Once the daily personal creativity flows smoothly and naturally, the person is ready to begin creative work in a professional setting.

Creating a habit of repetitively examining your mind

Again, what is creativity? It is an act or a state of mind when something new (for the creator) is made from something old. It may apply to new thoughts, theories, methods, or physical objects. The foundations of modern theories of creative thought were published for the first time by Graham Wallas in 1926, but since then, they have gone through multiple transformations and discussions.

Exercise: How would you discuss the theories of creative thought based on your insight?

Let me begin: Is creativity only a feature of (certain) humans? Maybe not. I recall my dog, who always found or made an escape route from a fenced yard; I can say that animals can be creative as well.

It was the beginning of the pandemic in 2020. While preparing my living room to make a video recording for teaching Tai Chi class via Zoom, I habitually observed whether this activity had any creative elements. While looking around at the well-known room and its furniture, my mind took various aspects and tried to visualize how to fit a yoga mat and a computer or a cellphone to make recordings. Having a few ideas, I unfolded the mat and checked the view with a camera. After testing a few spots, I saw that one is too bright, and another did not have enough distance for the camera. I was attempting to make a recording studio in my living room here. Taking old things and rearranging them to make something new, possibly unexpected and certainly not meant for such an event. I would address new circumstances and challenges by using things that I was familiar with. What fascinated me the most was creativity, the repetitive yet different challenge for the mind every time.

That was the time when I made my decision to write about creativity. My internal motivations were straightforward. I enjoyed observing creative thoughts daily in myself or the people around me. I saw that creativity was the solution to our highly diverse classroom. As a teacher, I faced challenges every day since my students came from many countries and represented various levels of growth. Thus, my reasons for writing were entirely selfish. Thinking and writing about creativity gave me an immense sense of joy. Moreover, I realized that staying with the topic of creativity made me more aware of creative flows that pass through my mind. Then, I could be more sensitive to creative flows through the minds of my students and mentees. Then, I could encourage their progress more insightfully. Thus, I would encourage other educators to observe and facilitate creativity.

Exercise: Write your motivations for developing creative vibes. Once they are well developed, how can they change you, your environment, your family, your job? What else could they change for you and others? Is that vision motivating?

Starting creative thinking in professional settings

Stepping out of the cozy space of privacy and experiencing creative vibes in the formal world of one's profession can initially be uncomfortable. However, over time, this experience can only get increasingly exhilarating.

While reflecting on the importance and necessity of being creative, I notice that almost everything we do either contains some elements of creativity or is a form of appreciation of it. While getting up from bed in the morning, I noticed someone had an idea of building a bed. Getting dressed is possible because someone had an idea of sawing pieces of fabric together to make clothing. While checking the weather on my cellphone, I appreciate the device, which results from the advanced creative thinking of generations of scientists. Reading books, I experience the vastness of the creative thoughts of the authors. The list of appreciations is endless.

Exercise: From various perspectives, make your daily lists of appreciations of creative thoughts and objects around you. How do these lists change from day to day?

Preparing creative assignments

I like to let students know that their questions in class, their comments, and our class discussions inspire me to create class activities that, I hope, address students' needs in the best possible ways. This attitude formally shifts the responsibility of the class's shape toward the students' side, and their reactions are always very encouraging. Then, the creation of class activities becomes co-creation, which is collaborative work between the students and the teacher. The class becomes much more exciting and engaging if students have a chance to provide responsible feedback and opinions. A few years ago, encouraged by my students, I began using class worksheets. Every semester, I would seek feedback from students about possible modifications, always emphasizing that the current shape results from honest feedback and solicited support from previous semesters. Similarly, all creative assignments in my classes are assisted by generous students' feedback and reflections.

Students are already creative in their ways

This may be surprising to some, but students of all ages, moreover, all people, are (or were) creative in their ways. This must be recognized and valued before any creativity in the classroom begins.

Recently, in my class, I asked students about creativity. We briefly discussed the definitions of creativity and spoke about the value of encouraging creativity. We all agreed that life during the pandemic required multiple adjustments, allowing us to be creative daily. Then, students submitted their writing on Blackboard Discussion, answering a few questions already discussed in class. One was: In what ways are you creative, and what inspires you? Most students claimed they were very creative, some mentioned their creativity was relatively minor, and only one person (out of 15) claimed they were entirely not creative. Here are a few samples from students' work compiled together into one quote:

> "I think I only get creative when I take pictures. The
> beauty of nature always inspires me. I use creativity
> when I am playing basketball or when I am playing

video games with my friends because I want to be different. I think I am creative because I always have tricky thinking processes, and I like to think a lot. I think life can inspire me. Things that inspire me to be creative are things that I never expected or interest me. In baking, I use creativity to design different pastries. I instantly use my imagination to create ideas to create a design for shoes or t-shirts. What inspires me are things that are meaningful to me. I am a creative person when it comes to solving math problems. For example, if I get taught a certain way, I will try to be creative and find another easier way to solve a problem. Listening to music inspires me because it helps me relax and be calm. For example, my friend is a barber (he has to create several hairstyles a day on unique heads) and then makes music in his free time. What inspires me is seeing what other people can accomplish and thinking about how I could recreate what they have done differently or better. I can develop different ways of comprehending things while studying to help me remember better. I edit videos and have a podcast that I am very proud of. I make my shirts and shorts involving creativity to make a vision a reality. Things that inspire me are honestly the ocean; the ocean allows me to calm down and forget about the world, which helps me develop new ideas. One thing that I can do very well is to write mystery or thriller stories. I have such a crazy imagination when it comes to this that the stories I write can be excellent. I would love to learn more ways to influence myself and challenge my thinking into something else. I want to learn more about the mind by researching to become more familiar with it."

This list appears rather impressive and indicates that college students generally recognize creative activities, perform them, and draw certain happiness from them.

What do your students think about creativity?

While working on any project, I suggest that my students make a habit of checking their state of mind toward it and see whether it is like a "child playing around" without concern for the outcomes or a "shy teenager" claiming that this is not going to work, or a "calm student" writing a report because it needs to be done. Alternatively, maybe a mix of all of them taking turns. It is good to be aware of each state and the shifts between them. More importantly, students are encouraged to define their states of mind according to their taste and their observations.

While making a progress on a path to a creative mind, one may wonder what others think about creativity, particularly their own creativity. I often had a chance to discuss creative attitudes with my students without a clear conclusion about their thoughts since the reflections strongly depended on the circumstances and the way of asking. However, overall, I thought that it was necessary to ask.

How to ask

There are numerous methods to introduce students to creative assignments in class. It is essential to address the changes, explain the concept of creativity for education, mention your curiosity toward the topic, and explain the collaborative nature of it. In my case, I explain that I am a researcher of creativity since I pay attention to the process of thoughts, discuss it with my colleagues, write and read about it. This is a natural continuation of my interest in the process of thinking and growth of my students because teaching mathematics requires specific insight into students' mistakes. Since the mind spontaneously generates errors, it is worthwhile to closely examine how it functions during study and learning.

It is imperative to give a brief description of examples of creative adventures. However, this may be challenging at the very beginning of the journey. Usually, I give examples of my collaborative projects with students and explain how they were created as natural extensions of classroom assignments. In the presentation of creativity to students, I like mentioning that creativity is a natural feature of the human mind, very distinguished in the case of children but regrettably forgotten during the process of maturation and classroom (over)memorization. My favorite part is to talk about the stages of creativity and give examples of the Illumination stage as described by Hugo Steinhaus, a mathematician from the Lwów School of Mathematics, who claimed to have an illuminating thought while opening the door to his house (Steinhaus, 2024). This picture of opening the door symbolizes the mysterious Illumination stage since it is the moment when creative thought passes from the subconscious mind through a mental barrier to the conscious mind. I often give more examples of my own or my students' Illumination moments related to my very recent projects. My memory of excitement, delight, and enthusiasm packed in those moments is essential in this subconscious message.

To give an example of a project with a long-term creative flow, I mention a project about solar panels' geometry (and other features). Over many years, multiple groups of students have built up their new ideas after reading previous students' work. Since they wrote neatly organized reports and later converted them to conference papers every year, it is easy for new groups to pick up on a modified theme and continue the work of their peers.

After providing firsthand examples of creative thoughts and flows, I ask students whether they are creative and what inspires them. They are also asked to give examples of creative thoughts or creative flows that they recently experienced. This question is usually immediately answered affirmatively by students who do artwork or creative writing while others remain silent. However, a written part of this assignment reveals that more students perform creative works, recognize them, and value them.

What to say

My classes frequently discuss "The 16 Habits of mind" (Costa & Kallick, 2000). Fortunately, the list of habits includes creativity (Creating, imagining, and innovating) and mind plasticity (Thinking flexibly). It is an everyday activity for the students to watch various videos to grasp the subject better. Usually, I select a few presentations about creativity and a few about plasticity among TED talks. Then, I "coincidentally" present these two topics together. After watching each presentation, students answer basic questions about the presenters, the topics, and the central claims. Students are asked to respond to a few prompts during a discussion preceding the videos. Before watching the presentation about the plasticity of the mind, students are asked whether they could shape their minds and to what extent. During the talk, the presenter mentioned that our responsibility is to shape our minds, which is a fundamental observation yet difficult to understand for some students.

Students' responses

During the written assignment summarizing the lesson, students were asked to reflect on the following prompts: Do you think you will need to be creative in the future? At work and in daily life? Do you value creative thinking? If you could, would you shape yourself into an innovator?

Likely, the video presentations and discussions performed immediately before writing influenced students' responses. Here is an analysis of what

75

students wrote. The following is a compilation of submissions from eleven students (thus anecdotal, not statistically significant by any means). What drew my attention is that all students elaborated on these straightforward questions, matching them with their worlds of reasons and values. I can sense that they did not copy their answers from any internet source but wrote straight from their hearts and minds.

As expected, all students think they will need creativity in the future but express it differently, providing various reasons why it is helpful for them. Some mention financial benefits, success, and simply moving up the ladder. Some values impact society, such as earning fame with creative ideas or simply being noticed.

Others focus on discovering their passion, expressing themselves as humans or artists, and being better or unique. Some say creativity can help them realize their purpose, live exciting lives, or create interesting artwork. Some students claim that creative thinking can help them in challenging situations, making their family life easier even with advanced technology. Other students see creativity as benefiting future generations by creating something new and valuable or developing a good strategy for creating new solutions to old problems. Someone saw a value in figuring out new ways of thinking that were nonexistent before and not available to others.

Interestingly, one student from an engineering major claimed that he is not creative since he always looks at things analytically and uses logic to back up his reasoning.

As expected, all students claim that they value creative thinking and are willing to put their minds to work to see things differently, be helpful to people, and pass the results of their work on to future generations.

The discrepancy within the group happens when students start thinking of shaping their minds into innovators. Even within such a small group, some students refuse that option, some are uncertain about it, and others are ready to try. The one student who refuses motivates his position by not being innovative and preferring to follow others' guidance, never trying to change things or making anything new.

These few uncertain students motivate their position in different ways. One already knows methods for being creative but sometimes prefers guidance from others and does not see himself as an independent creator in all situations. Another student says he may become an innovator but does not comment further. There is one response where a student says he would like to shape himself into an innovator because he is not creative enough. Coincidentally, another student gave the exact reason for not trying to be innovative. The same observation may influence different students in entirely divergent ways. Most of my students expressed their interest in shaping themselves into innovators. Regardless of their actual insight into the process of doing so and their skills in implementing that insight, these students consciously expressed their wish to transform themselves into creative beings. Again, their motivation ranged from financial, self-improvement, being a better engineer, curiosity, learning new things, and trying themselves. One student expressed his interest in "being his own person."

How will you introduce creativity in your classes? How will you speak with students about it? How will you collect their responses and admit their existing creativity?

Riding the Bull Home

Mounting the Ox, slowly
I return homeward.
The voice of my flute intones
through the evening.
Measuring with hand-beats
the pulsating harmony,
I direct the endless rhythm.
Whoever hears this melody
will join me.

—6—

Lectures and Projects

Since introducing creative ideas in professional work may carry some initial doubt or anxiety, it is wise to start small and then slowly increase the caliber and scope of creative ideas. I would suggest starting outside the regular classroom and beginning a creative adventure during meetings of a math club or another informal lecture. Such venues foster more relaxed and friendly atmosphere, promoting positive interactions between participants and the speaker. Furthermore, the audience differs from that in a regular classroom as it consists of self-selected individuals who are often deeply committed to their self-education. They seek learning outside the traditional classroom and are more supportive of new ideas, including new learning styles.

In my case, I began searching for topics and giving presentations for undergraduate students who attended the math club while still a PhD candidate at Missouri University of Science and Technology. My early themes circled around the enigma machines and modern encryption techniques with elliptic curves. These topics were equally attractive to both computer science students and engineering students. The only thing I still regret is that I did not begin such presentations earlier, possibly as a high school student. From today's perspective, I somehow missed an opportunity to grow my creativity skills early in my professional career.

Keeping in mind that redesigning an entire course to introduce creative aspects to the curriculum may be more challenging and time-consuming, but preparing a lecture for a broad audience with creative elements sounds like an engaging and fun beginning of a journey of creative mind, I placed the chapter with creative projects before the chapter with creative classroom assignments. Here, the reader will find various topics and approaches that will hopefully inspire their own explorations. The chapter begins with some suggestions on approaching the idea of creative projects. After reflecting on my observations, I gathered essential aspects that, in my opinion, lead to successful and enriching projects.

1. Begin informal conversations to find interesting topics for students and you. Ask for students' majors, hobbies, interests, free time activities, and names of coffee shops (grocery stores, streets, cafeterias, bookstores, libraries, etc.) nearby. Engage a small group of students in a discussion about their plans, goals, dreams, and, more importantly, their impossible dreams. One of my students said she would like to work on a project combining calculus and civil engineering, which sparked a discussion of how transparent, flexible solar panels could be placed on buildings of various shapes. This inspired multiple research topics and multiple publications for many years.

2. On a regular (daily or weekly) basis, exchange useful links via group emails, Blackboard resources, Google Docs, or others. Use Google

Hangouts or other platforms to facilitate the flow of creative thoughts applied to even small inquiries. For example, while watching NASA TV, my students had numerous questions about basic science; in particular, students investigated what NASA space technology is used in daily life. Later, their questions inspired prompts for essays assigned to other students. Receive suggestions and suggest readings to discuss them later in follow-up informal conversations. There is no need to be teacher-centered since the students can inspire one another.

3. Search for open problems with students and encourage them in their approach. Following a student's intuition may appear nonscientific but often leads to unexpected results since students' minds are fresh and not biased by previous experience. Do not be afraid to launch a project in a research area that is new to you, as this will allow you to learn alongside your students.

4. Check time availability and other commitments. Students enrolled in excessive classes or handling full-time jobs may still be willing to commit to a project, but time management may be quite challenging. It may be wise to invite students for an informal short-term learning project before inviting them into a formal long-term research project to acclimatize them to the time required to complete a research project.

5. Use group work and internal peer review so that students can critique and challenge the thinking of their peers and be allowed to communicate and justify their thinking. It will take care of students' misjudgments and misunderstandings of the level of expectations. At the same time, small mistakes are corrected while the observant students receive applause for finding others' errors.

6. For similar reasons, encourage students to participate in undergraduate conferences and present their work informally and formally in various

formats. Preparing posters, slides, essays, and papers allows the students to see their work from different perspectives. Students may get very excited about such opportunities and see them as a way to improve their communication skills. This is particularly important for non-native English speakers.

7. Give certificates after the completion of the project and congratulatory letters after each published paper, presentation, or poster display. Stay in touch with your research students even if their participation was minor; offer to write letters of support and encourage further growth.

Exercise: In your opinion, what steps lead to successful research projects for students? How do you imagine your collaboration with students outside of the classroom? How would you select students for the projects? Or should you allow students to make such decisions on their own? Would you ask students what topics and styles of work they prefer?

As stated and verified in (Russell & et al, 2007) and (Hackett & et al, 1992), student participation in undergraduate research projects positively influences their performance in further development, academic skills, GPA, and writing skills. It improves students' retention in STEM disciplines whether their participation is based on their willingness or is mandatory, as in (Nadga & et al, 1998). On my side, I found that students who completed the projects gained true self-esteem and matured. Students' statements about the benefits of joining the projects are compiled below.

Before formally joining the projects, students described their expectations in personal statements and talked about their careers, improving professional skills, and personal feelings and goals. Here are some statements from students' essays,

"One benefit will be better understanding what 'doing research' actually means."

"Hopefully, through this research, I can discover a passion and continue to graduate studies shortly."

"Ideally, my goal is to combine my love for architecture with my strong STEM skills to solve urban problems. I believe that relating these two passions with calculus will enforce my understanding of the material and could therefore apply it later on in my career as an engineer."

"Furthermore, this research experience will allow me to understand published works better, learn to balance collaborative and individual work, and determine an area of interest."

Since I began mentoring students, my organizational and personal skills have significantly improved, and my research in mathematics and pedagogy has reached a higher level. It became more about communicating skillfully - more about "how" and less about "what."

In my classes, I announce an opportunity to work on a research project and observe how students' attitudes change towards the course when the topics open doors to mysterious new worlds and unknown problems for everybody, not only the selected research students.

Exercise: What are the benefits of incorporating creative students' projects into the college curriculum? Do you think that you will benefit from those projects? How would the students benefit?

Spirograph

My long-term project with the Spirograph began in 2015 when I bought the complete set to display during a college math event. Since the toy was appreciated by students who asked insightful math questions, I decided to prepare a lecture about this topic with hands-on activities. During the first lecture, students played with the toy and saw the formulas used to draw the spirograph curves, along with the Mathematica demonstration. They tried to answer multiple questions, such as: How does the ratio of the radii of the two circles influence the shape of the curve? Can it happen that the curve never ends?

In the meantime, my classrooms transformed, and I began introducing historical and linguistic backgrounds for some lectures. Since my students' reactions were very positive, I included this aspect in the spirograph lecture and mentioned the first drawing devices and their purposes.

On the other hand, my artistic side saw a chance to digitally create beautiful images of curves with fancy colors and backgrounds with Mathematica. A few times, I displayed them in my classes, and students immediately expressed their interest in visual arts and programming. This was mainly designed for non-math students who declare that they do not like math and consider it useless for their future.

Recently, I had a chance to present a lecture about the Spirograph to students and faculty of another college. Such lectures are equally demanding and rewarding to prepare since they must entertain a diverse audience of laypeople and high-caliber professionals. The exposition was expanded by a list of open-ended questions and an attempt to solve one of them. The lecture aimed to demonstrate how a game can be a source of inspiration for advanced mathematical research.

Here is a sample lecture developed over a few years for college events. The presentation begins just like any lecture for a broad audience, with a few historical and epistemological remarks to entertain the audience. At the same time, they play with the Spirograph, maybe for the first time after a long break. Here is a brief lecture synopsis adjusted for a broad college audience.

Lecture: Math Problems Motivated by the Spirograph

I suppose that the audience consists mainly of students who, due to the rigid structure of mathematics instructions, think that everything in mathematics is already discovered, set in stone, and never changing. Today, I would like to demonstrate that this stereotype is mistaken by presenting how a simple drawing toy such as the Spirograph can inspire open-ended math questions that anybody can think about.

In 1827 English architect and engineer Peter Hubert Desvignes developed his "Speiragraph," a machine to create elaborate spiral drawings to prevent bank note forgeries. Modern Spirograph was developed by a British engineer, Denys Fisher, and sold for the first time in 1965. In 2013, Kahootz Toys relaunched the brand. However, the curves drawn by the Spirograph have an even more extended history.

The simplest case of a circle rolling along a line is called a cycloid, named "The Helen of Geometers," since it was the reason for quarrels among 17th-century geometers. Math historians claim that this curve has been known and studied since antiquity. In another case, when a circle rolls along another circle (inside or outside), it can produce a variety of shapes that depend on the ratio of their radii. In the case of rational ratios, the resulting curve ends where it began. However, in irrational ratios, the resulting curve can be drawn infinitely long since it never ends. While drawing on paper with a thick pencil, we may not notice that and simply think that the curve and when the lines slightly overlap, but mathematically, assuming infinite thinness of the drawing line, we can continue until infinity.

Let us begin thinking creatively. In mathematics, we often generalize and turn old concepts into new directions. Let me see how the concept of drawing rolling curves could be expanded. Do not worry about judgment since this is supposed to be fun, and whatever you invent is acceptable.

In the Spirograph, a CIRCLE ROLLS along another CURVE, which is often but not necessarily a circle. Moreover, there is a drawing point on the PLANE. Let us try to relax one of these aspects and check whether we can visualize the situation:

- Could something else (not a circle) roll along a curve? What would that be? In mathematics, there are many different classes of curves that, in some sense, resemble a circle, such as closed curves or curves of constant width.

- Could a curve be rolled along another shape? What would that shape be? Could we roll along the surface? Which direction?

- Is the Spirograph possible in a higher dimensional space or on a curved manifold?

- Could we replace the rolling motion with another motion? What would that be?

- We mentioned a fixed choice of a point, but could the point move within a circle with a specific pattern? What pattern? Should we consider choosing a smudging shape instead of a point? Like a brush or a marker?

Here is the explanation of a solution to one of those questions using analogy with the original solution. Let us try to generalize the formulas to higher dimensions. Let $\vec{r}(s)$ parametrize the space curve A by its length with $\vec{T}(s)$ and $\vec{N}(s)$, the tangent and the normal vectors, respectively. If a denotes the radius of the rolling circle C, Then, its center, as it rolls on A is parameterized by $\vec{r}(s) \pm a\,\vec{T}(s)$. The sign depends on the orientation of A and on the side, the circle is rolling. The trouble may happen when the tangent vector is equal to zero but with an assumption that A is smooth, we can avoid that trouble. For singular curves, we would choose piecewise formulas. If b denotes the distance between the drawing point and the center of the rolling circle, then note that with $a = b$ the drawing point is on the edge. With $a < b$ the drawing point is outside of the circle, and with $a > b$ the drawing point is inside the circle. Choosing a value of $t \in [0, \pi]$ give a phase shift to the drawing point. Then, the parametrization of the drawn curve B is as follows:

$$\vec{R}(s) = \vec{r}(s) \pm a\,\vec{T}(s) + b\Big(\cos(t-s)\vec{T}(s) + \sin(t-s)\,\vec{N}(s)\Big).$$

Figure. A sample curve sketched by a Spirograph

Exercise: As a college instructor, consider presenting your lecture for a math club or a program within your or a sister college. As a high school teacher, you can present for another school. I bet that neighboring schools are always looking for speakers. As a student, you could make your presentation for a math club at a lower-level school. Consider discussing the themes with possible audiences while searching for suitable topics, places, and venues. What are they interested in? Modern technology? Or maybe old technology used in modern devices? Or some surprising applications in daily devices? Or is the audience entirely oriented towards abstract mathematics? I bet that you have already been working on something like this. Searching old thumb drives and floppy discs may reveal some forgotten notes that may inspire new creative works.

BEAG (Beginners Explorations of Algebraic Geometry)

My colleagues frequently act as motivators for creative activities. In 2017, during a conversation with two of my colleagues, we observed that many mathematics seminars we attended in the past followed an unappealing format where the speaker projected her work on the board without much concern for audience understanding. Thus, we invented a seminar that included free explorations. We decided every meeting should contain hands-on assignments where seminar participants can get their hands dirty with simple examples. Such a form proved to be relatively easy for the speaker to accomplish but quite challenging for the participants. We have been consistently following this idea since 2017 and enjoying a variety of topics and a variety of hands-on assignments. While exploring the topic of elliptic curves, we realized that we could study dynamics on elliptic curves. We discovered it while sketching examples of elliptic curves, and while sketching their Hessians, we observed cycles. Then, we began wondering whether such cycles were standard or if it was pure luck. We invited a colleague specializing in complex dynamics to teach us about the subject. The colleague was quite excited about our discovery since he was longing for examples of dynamics in other areas of mathematics.

Exercise: Are your co-workers interested in supporting creative assignments? Could any of them join your path of creative work?

Would they appreciate their participation? Would they cheer up your progress? In times of remote activities, such collaborators could be far away in space and share their progress on that topic.

Game of Cycles

I was introduced to the Game of Cycles during the ICERM workshop, which took place in June 2019. It was a joint effort of the entire group, which resulted in the article "Game of Cycles" published in the American Mathematical Monthly (Alvarado, Averett, & et al, 2021). The game is elementary, with rules that can be explained to a child, but at the same time, it leads to nontrivial investigations of the strategies. Here is a brief description of the game and possible research questions that will be enjoyable for students and professional mathematicians.

Consider a connected planar graph and two players who mark the edges in one direction without creating sinks (vertices only with edges "in") or sources (vertices only with edges "out"). The winner is the player who makes the last available move or creates a "cell cycle." A cell cycle differs from a graph cycle by embracing an actual plane region.

The game also has its interpretation of a real-life problem as it resembles a process of converting a graph into a digraph. This is the same as redesigning a city's road map from two-way to one-way streets. The vertices are interpreted as intersections, and the edges are streets. The assumption that no sinks and no sources are allowed means no intersections with streets exclusively in or streets exclusively out. The players' roles and the winning strategy can be omitted in this interpretation. However, another problem becomes more relevant: for which game boards (street designs) exist a traffic design that uses exclusively one-way streets? In the game terminology, we express it as having no unmarkable edges.

Here are a few questions similar to those posed in the article:

1. Which graphs are interesting to play on? Here, interesting means that there are no winning strategies for either player, or they are non-trivial.
2. Conversely, one can ask which graphs have obvious winning strategies.
3. The game could be altered in many ways; for example, one could play on a space graph, an infinite, or with multiple players. Which alterations are interesting for the questions above?

Exercise: Even such a simple game can serve as an inspiration for research work. Search for more such games. Alter the rules or goals and prepare questions for creative students' work.

Mathematics of Energy

It is not a mystery that mathematics appears in many other areas. Sometimes, the same mathematical phenomena appear in different disciplines to express the same "forces of nature" in different mediums. Here is a project that can be broadly classified as social sciences with varied mathematics content.

Project: Mathematics of Energy

Math Topics: Space Curves, Surfaces

Math Level: Calculus 3

During the winter of 2015-16, three students from my Calculus 3 class expressed their interest in developing internal knowledge to relate subjective and objective signs of being tired or energized. They analyzed the physiology of their body (pulse and the number of breaths per minute) in relationship to a subjective feeling of energy. Such objective data (and even more) can now be collected via a smartwatch, which makes the project even more available to students. The three quantities could be represented as points on a space curve if time is treated as a parameter or points on a surface if time is omitted. The techniques of representation belong to the curriculum of Calculus 3, but tools from statistics may also be used to study the correlations among these quantities. Students recorded their data individually over one week. Three times a day, students measured their pulses, counted the number of breaths per minute, and then (subjectively) rated their energy levels on a scale of 1 through 10. While doing the project and recording the data, they reached some insightful conclusions about their energy levels.

Assignment: A person's pulse and the number of breaths per minute are objective quantities, and the person's energy level is subjective. The project aims to find connections between subjective and objective quantities.

Student work:

1. Collect the data about these quantities thrice daily (or more frequently) over one week. Use the energy level from the range of 1 to 10, assuming that 0 is when you are asleep and do not collect the data.

2. Visualize your data using seven curves (one for each day) with parameter t as time. What patterns do you observe?

3. Visualize your data using points with three coordinates. What patterns do you observe?

4. What observations about yourself did you make during the data collection week? In particular, do you see a relationship between your feeling of energy and your pulse or the number of breaths per minute?

Exercise: Perform the measurements to get a grip on the assignment. What alterations would you apply to make the assignment more appealing to your students? However, at the same time, it should remain within the scope of the courses you are teaching. Data can be visualized in many ways. What ways are suitable for your courses?

Chromatherapy

Lecture: Influence of light color on mood and perception

Here is a sample lecture about a topic not necessarily aligned with my professional education in mathematics but is very much aligned with my passion for self-observation and self-assessment. The idea for a lecture resulted from discussions with a co-worker interested in creating interdisciplinary projects that connect computer science and psychology. She knew about my interests in meditation and specific experiments with color light to alert one's moods and wanted to encourage me to do more in that direction. This lecture was part of a sequence of lectures where faculty from various departments prepared interdisciplinary projects for students who programmed a Raspberry PI.

What is light? We can treat it for this presentation as wavelengths in the range of 400-700 nanometers. The frequency determines the light color. Monochromatic light or small bandwidth light consists of wavelengths of similar frequency. Polychromatic light contains wavelengths of multiple frequencies. The color we perceive is determined mainly by the relative contributions of blue, green, and red cones to the retinal signal. The fact that our visual system detects colors in this way was predicted by a British physicist, Thomas Young, who showed in 1802 that all the colors of the rainbow, including white, could be created by mixing the proper ratio of red, green, and blue light (RGB). He proposed that at each point in the retina, a cluster of three receptor types exists, each being maximally sensitive to either blue, green, or red. Hermann von Helmholtz, an influential nineteenth-century German physiologist, later championed Young's ideas.

The retina contains photoreceptors that convert light energy into neural activity. Cones are responsible for color vision. In 1965, experimental confirmation came that there were three color-sensitive cones: L, M, and S, corresponding roughly to red, green, and blue sensitive detectors. Since the discovery of intrinsically photosensitive retinal ganglion cells (ipRGCs) in the human eye, many studies have been conducted to investigate the non-image-forming effects of ocular light exposure on human functioning during the biological night and day. Research has established that light does not only have the potential to produce phase-shifting effects on the human circadian rhythm but can also exert instantaneous effects on physiological arousal, neural activity, hormone production, and subjective alertness. In addition, light has also been shown to impact cognitive ability, including attention, inhibitory control, and working memory. The main issue with the research results related to the perception of light colors is low statistical significance and difficulties confirming the results. It may be due to the highly individualized perception of light colors performed by the brain (not the retina). This highly individualized perception may be created when the vision develops in a child. This depends on the location, the weather, and the culture of staying outdoors or indoors with closed curtains.

Thus, we propose a project to verify the variability of preferences towards light colors.

The project consists of two parts:

1. Self-observation of preferences towards various light colors during activities such as studying, thinking, reading, falling asleep, resting, relaxing, reading, and more. Assessment of how light colors influence the success in studying,

2. The programming aspect of the project is where students program a device with Raspberry PI to obtain selected light colors and control their intensity.

More about this topic can be found in (Rua, de Kortb, & et al, 2019), in (Bear, Connors, & et al, 2006) and in the paper written with my student Julissa Cardoza (Cardoza & Marciniak, 2024).

Exercise: Changing the colors of the surrounding light may genuinely alter one's perception and mood. To test your sensitivity to light color, repeat one of the previous exercises to note various ideas that come to your mind. Can you observe any differences in your perception? How about other aspects of your environment? Is there something around you that inspires your creativity? Or something that discourages your creativity?

Modeling Caffeine Levels

Once the ideas bloom, it may be time to compose a class project, where students need to think about open non-mathematical questions based on math calculations. The most natural type of project consists of gathering data, representing it, and performing calculations, reflections, and discussions.

Project: Caffeine Level and sleep disruption

Math Topic: Exponential Decay

Math Level: Precalculus

The need for this assignment came from the departmental requirement for applied class projects, where students work on problems related to their daily lives. The challenge of such projects in developmental math courses comes from the limited mathematical tools students can use. Moreover, such a project should address a particular topic, which, in this case, is exponential decay. In my first idea, I wanted students to observe a melting cube to find the exponential decay parameters. However, it was clear that nobody would care about melting ice cubes, so I began searching for a topic more significant to students. Inspiration for this topic arrived at the college when I noticed a student from my class drinking a large cup of coffee in the late afternoon. I spoke with the student, inquiring whether she experiences sleep disruption. Upon returning to my office, I checked the models for caffeine levels in the body and discovered that the models were based on exponential decay. Then, I realized this was precisely the topic I had been searching for. Exponential decay appears in many situations and is crucial for understanding the level of medications for students of all medical degrees (nursing, pharmacy, dentistry, veterinary, etc.).

The process of developing the final version of the project was quite lengthy. It involved accommodating feedback from faculty members with different specialties, including mathematics, engineering, computer science, health sciences, natural sciences, social sciences, and English. I am deeply thankful for all these contributions, which shaped the final version of the project.

Objectives: While working on this project, students will learn exponential functions in the context of the half-life of caffeine. In addition, students will reflect on caffeine levels in their bodies as a source of potential benefits and dangers. This project is especially suitable for medical science students.

Guidelines: This project is directed to students who drink coffee or intake caffeine products or have family members who do so and are willing to participate in collecting the data. Students will create groups of 2-3, making sure that at least one person in each group can collect the appropriate information. The written report will be created by each student, either in the first person or in the third person, depending on whether a student is writing about their own experience, a colleague's, or a family member's experience.

Caffeine is a substance that occurs naturally in a variety of food products, such as coffee, tea, and cocoa. Consuming is a daily habit of many adults since caffeine can stimulate the nervous system. The Journal of Food and Science suggested 400 mg as the maximum safe level of caffeine for an adult, but in the case of pregnancy, the safe level drops to 100 mg.

The kidneys filter the blood and remove caffeine and other drugs through urination. The time taken for a substance to fall to half its original value is called the half-life. The biological half-life of caffeine is approximately 6 hr. If one cup of coffee has 80 mg of caffeine, then the amount of caffeine C (in mg) remaining after t hours is given by the following exponential decay formula:

$$C = 80 \cdot 2^{\frac{-t}{6}}.$$

The amount of caffeine in the blood can be treated as a function of time. This universal formula looks similar to prescription drugs with possibly different half-times. Most people feel energized if the caffeine level is above 60 mg but may have difficulties falling asleep if the caffeine level is above 30 mg.

After time t hours a drink with initial C_0 mg of caffeine provides $C(t)$ mg of caffeine in the blood:

$C(t) = C_0 \cdot 2^{\frac{-t}{6}}$. High levels of caffeine may cause sleep disruption. What is your caffeine level at the moment of sleep? This project will help you answer this question.

ASSIGNMENT 1: Collecting Data

1. Check the link below for caffeine content in various drinks. In case your drink does not appear on the list, use approximation. https://cspinet.org/eating-healthy/ingredients-of-concern/caffeine-chart

2. Record the times and amounts for each caffeine intake during the day (feel free to add more intakes if appropriate). Suppose you drink only one cup of coffee per day. In that case, you can add an occasional or hypothetical second cup in the afternoon to monitor possible levels of caffeine and its effects on you.

3. What time do you plan to sleep? Calculate the time (in hours) between each caffeine intake and your time of sleep:
Calculate the amount of caffeine from each intake at your time of sleep using the formula

$$C(t) = C_0 \cdot 2^{\frac{-t}{6}}.$$

4. Your total amount of caffeine at your sleep time is the sum of the amounts above.

SAMPLE ANALYSIS OF GATHERED EVIDENCE

Let us assume that someone drinks a cup of coffee with *100 mg* of caffeine while waking up at 6 am (time. $t = 0$) and then at 1 pm (time $t = 7\ hrs$) They have another coffee with *60 mg* of caffeine. When do they reach the level of *30 mg*? Without performing calculations, we can read from the graph below that at about midnight ($t = 18\ hrs$) the level of caffeine drops below *30 mg*.

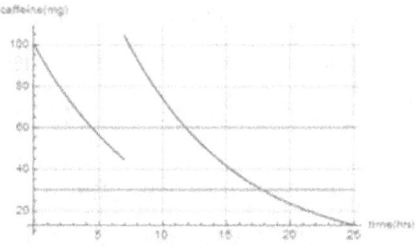

Figure. The graph of caffeine level after drinking a cup of coffee with 100 mg of caffeine at 6 am and a cup of coffee with 60 mg of caffeine at 1 pm

Now, let us add one more caffeinated drink. Someone drinks a cup of coffee with *100 mg* of caffeine while waking up at 6 am (time. $t = 0$) then at 1 pm (time $t = 7 \ hrs$) they have another coffee with *60 mg* of caffeine and later at 6 pm (time $t = 12 \ hrs$) they have another coffee with *60 mg* of caffeine. When do they reach the level of *30 mg*?

Without performing calculations, we can read from the graph that at midnight ($t = 18 \ hrs$) the level of caffeine is *60 mg*. The level of caffeine reaches *30 mg* at 6 am the next day ($t = 24 \ hrs$). It is time to get up!

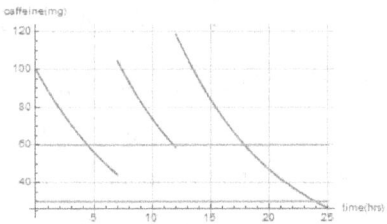

Figure. The graph of caffeine level after drinking a cup of coffee with 100 mg of caffeine at 6 am, a cup of coffee with 60 mg of caffeine at 1 pm, and then a cup of coffee with 60 mg of caffeine at 6 pm

The graphs presented here were made with mathematical software. After opening Maple, start a new worksheet and type the following command to produce the graph from above:

98

plot([100*2^(-t/6)+60*2^(-(t-6)/6)*Heaviside(t-6)+60*2^(-(t-12)/6)*Heaviside(t-12), 60, 30], discont=true)

Each term in the sum indicates one caffeine intake. The first one with 100 mg is taken at time t = 0 and is typed as 100*2^(-t/6). The second one, 6 hours later with 60 mg, is typed as 60*2^(-(t-6)/6)*Heaviside(t-6). The last one, with 60 mg, 12 hours later, is typed as 60*2^(-(t-12)/6)*Heaviside(t-12).

A graphic calculator can perform a similar task. Here is a link to a YouTube tutorial for graphing piecewise functions with a TI-84 calculator (https://www.youtube.com/watch?v=oHyoe60 mg? When is it below 30 mg?RsSH0g).

You could use these graphs to monitor the level of caffeine in your body, which would help you excel on all your tasks but still get enough rest, making sure that at the moment of sleep, your caffeine level is below 30mg.

Note that the next day does not begin with the level of caffeine equal to 0. Thus, our calculations for the previous day were not precise since the previous day possibly carried the initial level of caffeine equal to a nonzero amount inherited from the day before yesterday.

ASSIGNMENT 2: Analysis of gathered evidence.

Using Maple, another software, or a graphic calculator, represent your data on a graph and based on it, respond to the following questions.

Briefly describe your caffeine habits. Are you a frequent or occasional coffee (tea) drinker? How would you describe the influence of coffee on your energy level throughout the day? Does coffee help you with your daily tasks?

Analyze the graph of your caffeine level from the following perspective: When is your caffeine level above 60 mg?

ASSIGNMENT 3: Framing an issue.

Declare the purpose of this project, the process of collecting the data, and the analysis. Do you think your sleep is or is not affected by caffeine?

ASSIGNMENT 4: Drawing conclusions supported by evidence.

If you would make adjustments in your caffeine intake, how would you justify them? Or how would you justify your decision for not making any adjustments?

Did you find this project engaging? Are you interested in researching caffeine levels and their influence on people? Would you like to optimize caffeine intake for optimal performance without causing sleep disruption? Reflecting on this topic may help your career path, especially if you major in natural sciences or nursing.

Exercise: Finding the topic of this project resulted from an association that took place during a simple walk around the campus. What do you think about while walking inside and outside the campus buildings? Do you observe? Do you associate the observations with your classes? How could those observations help you be creative in the classroom? Do you speak with your students about their habits?

Modeling insulin and sugar levels

While introducing the previous project related to the level of caffeine in the body, I heard students suggest that those who do not drink coffee could instead analyze changes in their sugar and insulin levels. However, it turned out that the mathematical model of sugar metabolism is much more complicated than exponential decay. Since high sugar levels motivate insulin production and high levels of insulin lower the sugar levels, the model resembles a pendulum. Additional challenges are related to the necessity of using specialized tests to measure sugar levels, which is uncommon among math instructors. Thus, this project requires collaborative work among faculty and students from multiple areas. As I learned, testing the actual level of insulin is not in the hands of the college laboratory; therefore, in this project, the actual insulin levels can only be obtained based on a mathematical model.

Project: Insulin and sugar levels

Math Topics: Systems of Ordinary Differential Equations

Math Level: Differential Equations

The mathematical idea is based on the article from 1964 by Eugene Ackerman (Ackerman & et al, 1964) where the authors develop a system of linear differential equations to model the level of glucose and insulin. The resulting differential equations and their solutions appear frequently in physics and engineering as pendulum equations. This coincidence may create enthusiasm among representatives of these disciplines. I have to admit that I have tried to read the article and understand the physiology behind the equations but failed miserably due to insufficient background knowledge. At the very moment when I was ready to give up, a pre-med student showed up in my office and declared a wish to collaborate on "some project relating to mathematics and biology." When I asked the students to explain the diagram from the paper with a sketch of sugar metabolism, the students performed the task effortlessly. Such a quick assignment immediately informed me about the students' high capacity to explain concepts to a broad audience.

The project's challenge for students is to determine the parameters of the resulting model for their own (or someone else's) metabolism under various conditions, such as rest, exercise, and stress during exam

101

sessions. In particular, students tested how stress hormones, including epinephrine and cortisol, impact blood pressure and the heart rate and then compared sugar metabolism with caffeine and without it. Students demonstrated their creativity while designing situations for experiments, which included testing during regular times of the semester and exam sessions, as well as testing before and after running up and down the stairs. In addition, students tested with and without coffee. The collected data was then compared to the solutions of the differential equation to determine the values of the model parameters.

Here is the development of the equations with the notation below:

- G glucose concentration, G' its derivative
- H insulin concentration, H' its derivative
- $l_1 H$ average rate of insulin removal independent of glucose
- l_2 the average rate of release of insulin by the pancreas and dependent on glucose
- $l_3 G$ net increase in the rate of release of insulin due to glucose
- $l_4 G$ average rate of glucose removal independent of insulin
- l_5 average rate of release of glucose into the blood
- $l_6 H$ net increase in the average rate of glucose removal dependent on insulin
- $I(t)$ rate of increase of blood glucose due to absorption from intestines

The system of first-order linear differential equations is provided as

$$H' = -l_1 H + l_3 G + l_2$$

$$G' = -l_6 H - l_4 G + l_5 + I(t)$$

The system can be converted to the following second-order differential equation:

$$G'' + (l_4 + l_1)G' + (l_4 l_1 + l_3 l_6)G = l_1 I(t) + I'(t)$$

and further to

$$G'' + 2\alpha G' + \omega_0^2 G = S(t)$$

The solution is described as follows:

$$G = G_F + Ae^{-at} \sin \omega t$$

Where G_F is a fasting blood glucose level, ω_0^2 is the „responsivity" related to the parameters l_4, l_1, l_3, l_6 representing the body's response, α is the independent rate of removal of glucose and insulin.

Most students' observations fit the solution with certain approximations, including observations of a slightly diabetic participant. However, something unexpected happened, which was quite eye-opening to all researchers. One of the students who worked on the project happened to be Muslim and did her measurements during Ramadhan. Her sugar level curve taken after 9 pm (when she was allowed to eat after sunset) did not match the shape of the solution. She repeated the experiment and collected the data to confirm that the sugar level curve simply did not match the model. Motivated by that, I had a closer look at the beginning of the paper to check again the model's assumptions. Then, I realized that the researchers admitted that only 80% of their collected data fit their model. Somehow, we were fortunate to hit the marginal spot and even be able to explain the reasons! After discussing the case with several researchers, we concluded that the body did not produce sufficient insulin due to the unusual time of her sugar intake. The solution became possibly of the type:

$$G = G_F + Ate^{-at} \sin \omega t.$$

Surprisingly, this function does not solve the differential equation we were studying. On one side, this discovery explained a marginal amount of data mentioned in the article, which did not fit in with the general model. On the other hand, it became a puzzle for natural sciences researchers and

103

another mathematical modeling problem. As a continuation of the project, students needed to find a differential equation solved by such a function. This is, for example, the fourth-order differential equation with double complex roots. It can be written down in the following form, but an explanation of its biological meaning remains a mystery:

$$G^{(4)} + 4\alpha G^{(3)} + 2(2\alpha^2 + \omega_0^2)G'' + 4\alpha\omega_0^2 G' + \omega_0^4 G = S_1(t).$$

It is evident that even a relatively simple project can be a source of creative joy and may result in open research questions across multiple disciplines.

Exercise: This project was created as a follow-up to the previous (about caffeine levels) project going one step beyond the previous topic. Among the existing projects, one can search for other extensions and generalizations. On the other hand, one could simplify more advanced projects to match topics covered in courses at lower levels. Would it be possible to combine both projects about caffeine level and sugar level? What would be the goal of such a new combined project?

Modeling Body Temperature

Similarly, as in the previous projects, students in this project relate mathematical equations and their own experiences. A student interested in sports worked on this project with a friend. They both did multiple tests before taking proper measurements. The student used a thermal camera (FLIR E6) and took photos of a friend running on a track. They tested their hypothesis that the body's temperature during running can be modeled with exponential growth. This hypothesis was proven false after the student plotted the measurements on the graph. Then, she recognized that the graph resembles the logistic model and matched the data with that model. This project could be performed without the thermal camera, and instead, one could use a laser thermometer or any temperature sensor.

Project: Mathematics of Sports

Math Topics: Logistics Growth (and Decay)

Math Level: Precalculus or Differential Equations

Equipment: temperature sensor, Thermal camera FLIR E6

The student redesigned the entire approach a few times after several failed data collection attempts. At first, she tried to use the temperature sensor and tape it to the body in various spots, but it simply did not stick due to sweat. Then, she learned to use a thermal camera to perform her measurements. In the final version, the students decided to model the legs' temperature but also took measurements for the face and the belly. This turned out to be a challenging task due to excessive sweating, which caused inaccuracy in the readings of the thermal camera. As the follow-up project, the student planned to test the temperature of the swimmers. However, it turned out that due to the low temperature of the water, the swimmers were not warming up significantly to perform suitable measurements.

Here are the equations of the logistic model:

- P is the temperature of the body (legs) measured in Celsius,
- T is the time measured in minutes,
- M is the maximum body temperature can be adjusted depending on the circumstances.
- k is a constant to be found in the process of calculations (approximations)

The differential equation gives the logistic model:

$$\frac{dP}{dT} = kP(M - P)$$

After using the separation of variables, one obtains

$$\int \frac{dP}{dT} = \int kP(M - P)$$

$$\frac{1}{M} \int \left(\frac{1}{P} + \frac{1}{M-P}\right) dp = \int k\,dt$$

$$\frac{1}{M} \ln \left|\frac{P}{M-P}\right| = kt + c$$

$$\ln \left|\frac{P}{M-P}\right| = M(kt + c)$$

$$\frac{P}{M-P} = e^{M(kt+c)}$$

$$P = e^{M(kt+c)}(M - P)$$

$$P = Me^{M(kt+c)} - Pe^{M(kt+c)}$$

$$P\left(1 + e^{M(kt+c)}\right) = Me^{M(kt+c)}$$

$$P(t) = \frac{Me^{M(kt+c)}}{1+e^{M(kt+c)}}$$

Which can be rewritten as:

$$P(t) = \frac{M}{1+e^{-Mc}e^{-Mkt}}$$

After using the data on the temperature of the legs obtained from the thermal camera, the student found out that the temperature can be approximated as follows:

$$P(t) = \frac{46}{1 + 0.4375e^{46(0.0054)t}}$$

After completing this part of the project, the students modeled the cooling process of the legs. While working on the project, the student realized the challenges of research and the limitations of the tools and the measurements. She described it as a discrepancy between the ideas and the practice.

Exercise: What other processes could be tested with a temperature sensor? Could students test their hypotheses related to the mathematical models describing those processes? Using a thermal camera gives excess information about the actual temperature distribution on the legs' surface. Such two-dimensional data could be used for a more advanced project in partial differential equations to model the temperature of the inside of the calf muscle. However, I have never pursued this topic further. Would you try?

Aerodynamics

I am particularly sentimental about aerodynamics since this topic was my first mentoring project. I was invited by my colleagues and learned a great deal from them. For me the project began in 2015 with calculations for the elliptic wing. It was the first time I had witnessed the preparation and revision of project assignments performed by my more experienced mentors. What impressed me the most was the students' enthusiasm and energy while working on the project. The project went through many versions and variations; in the meantime, we designed horizontal wind turbines (even 3D printed a blade) using Blade Element Momentum Theory. In the project's second round, we optimized them using the Genetics Algorithm. Later, we decided to change the topic to drones, which introduced additional challenges due to multiple motors.

Here are a few sample assignments in basic aerodynamics.

Title: Visualization of the lifting force
Math Topics: Vector Fields. Line Integrals
Math Levels: Calculus 3

While the question "Why do airplanes fly?" may sound childish, the answer is neither simple nor silly. What is particularly interesting is that the first airplanes were designed without theoretical knowledge about this phenomenon, and all wings of the early airplanes were designed based on simulations in wind tunnels. Before explaining how the wings lift themselves and the body of the plane, it is possible to visualize the force that lifts a cylinder using the stream functions. The flow around a non-rotating cylinder with radius a and center $(0,0)$ can be modeled by the following function.

$$\phi(x, y) = Ux + \frac{Ua^2x}{x^2 + y^2}$$

Here x and y are the cartesian coordinated on the plane and U denotes the velocity of the (horizontal) wind. However, when the cylinder starts rotating, the flow is described as:

$$\phi(x, y) = Ux + \frac{Ua^2x}{x^2 + y^2} + \frac{-\Gamma}{2\pi} arctan\left(\frac{y}{x}\right)$$

Where Γ is the circulation. These functions are obtained by solving a partial differential equation that may not be suitable for a student who has not completed a Differential Equations course. However, a student who has completed Multivariable Calculus and is familiar with partial derivatives can verify that these solutions satisfy the Laplace equation and the appropriate boundary conditions. Here are sample questions for students:

a) Use your favorite software to sketch the gradient vector field $\vec{V} = \nabla \phi$ around each cylinder using U = 50m/sec, a = 3m and Γ = 2m2/sec. Adjust the values of U, a , and Γ to observe the changing behavior of the

108

vector field. Remember to place the cylinder in your picture and sketch the vector fields around it, not inside.

b) For each cylinder, evaluate the integrals

$$\int_C \vec{V} \cdot d\vec{r}$$

where C is the circle with radius a and $\vec{V} = \nabla\phi$. Compare and explain the results of integration for each case: the non-rotating and the rotating cylinder.

c) Can you explain in your own words "What lifts the cylinder?"

Exercise: This problem can be assigned in many ways and with many questions. One could ask: Can the wings be flat, or is the airfoil cross-section significant for the airplanes? Airfoils are interesting for their own sake and can be modeled with the Joukawsky transform.

Title: Joukowsky transform

Math course: Calculus 3 or Complex analysis of a single variable

Airfoils are fascinating for their beauty and shapes. Some of them can be modeled based on a complex function.

Nikolay Yegorovich Joukowsky (Joukovsky) (1847-1921) was a Russian mathematician and a founding father of the modern aerodynamics (and hydrodynamics). The most amazing early application of a complex variable that influenced the history of the modern world was the Joukowsky Transform. It is essential to mention that Joukowsky worked on airfoils (cross sections of wings) between 1868 and 1921 (Joukowsky, 1912). During those years, creating a successful design of an airplane was a subject of competition for many groups of engineers and companies worldwide. After the first confirmed flight in 1903, the engineering world still struggled to make airplanes stable and controllable in the air. Wind tunnels were already known and widely used for researching wing designs. However, a wind tunnel cannot create or develop a theoretical background for new airfoils. It can only provide information about existing airfoils. Joukowsky Transform maps a circle into the shape of an airfoil together with the streamlines around it. This discovery became a groundbreaking engineering accomplishment of his time. An example of a Joukowsky Transform is:

$$f(z) = z + \frac{1}{z},$$

which maps into an airfoil a circle that encloses the point $z = -1$ and passes through the point $z = 1$. The concept is even more fascinating because the airflow around the circle maps into the airflow around the airfoil.

Question: Using the software of your choice, map the airflow around the cylinder (from the previous project) into an airflow around the airfoil. Carefully choose a circle that encloses the point. $z = -1$ and passes through the point $z = 1$. Then, changing the parameters of such a circle, observe the changes in the airfoil. Explain the limitations of such an approach.

Exercise: Other complex functions can be used to model beautiful images. They may display themselves due to typos in the formulas. Keep track of your typos and the resulting graph.

Title: Analysis of the wind speed
Math topics: Statistics

Wind energy has been used in human history for centuries. As described in (Hau, 2013) windmills with fabric sails were known in ancient China and Persia. Vertical and horizontal axis mills were widely used for milling grains, pumping water, and draining land. Choosing the right place was always an important question when locating the mill. As it is today, before deciding on the design of the wind turbine, it is mandatory to analyze the local wind.

Using an anemometer, one can collect suitable data near the college, preferably on the rooftop of a tall building, or use the data publicly available, for example, from http://www.ncdc.noaa.gov. As mentioned in (Hau, 2013) on p. 193, the wind speed x is distributed according to the Weibull function defined for $x > 0$ as:

$$f(x; \lambda, k) = \frac{k}{\lambda} \left(\frac{x}{\lambda}\right)^{k-1} e^{-\left(\frac{x}{\lambda}\right)}$$

Answer the following questions:

A. Visualize the data and observe whether there is noise or errors.

B. Match the annual (or seasonal) wind speed frequency distribution in your location with the Weibull distribution for $k = 2$ (this distribution is sometimes called Rayleigh distribution).

C. Compare two methods (for example, maximum likelihood and minimum mean square error) for finding the estimators of the parameter λ.

D. Visualize your results and explain which method is better and why.

Exercise: The wind speed is tricky and highly variable quantity, even among close-up locations. Use the data from two different measuring locations to compare the parameters of the distributions. Are they similar? Is it possible to detect differences in the parameters of the distribution? How could their similarity be measured?

More about this topic can be found in (Marciniak, Nechayeva, Przhebelskiy, & et al, 2017).

Geometry of Solar Panels

This project originated from informal and spontaneous discussions that took place during a break between classes. Students became curious about the geometry of flexible solar panels after learning that modern technology enables the solar cells to be printed even on paper, as described in (Barr & et al, 2001). After establishing a collegial relationship and identifying a mathematical topic that interested all of us, we began asking questions and posing problems. During the summer of 2016, two other students joined the team, and we worked on analyzing the sun's trajectory for various places on Earth during different seasons. Eventually, we could derive two versions of the equations, one in rectangular coordinates and the other in spherical coordinates. We all had to learn how photovoltaic cells work and what affects their efficiency.

We worked on a mathematical simulation of the efficiency of shaped panels at the North Pole since the sun's trajectory is relatively simple to write in spherical coordinates. So far, the project has generated multiple articles which discuss the topic from various points of view. The most spectacular is probably the most recent, (Maskal, Aboudiwan, & Marciniak, 2020) which analyzes the sun's trajectory as seen from the Moon.

Here are sample assignments about evaluating the accumulation of sunbeams.

Title: Geometry of solar panels

Math Topics: Curve parametrization, surface parametrization, surface integrals

Math Level: Calculus 3

Assume that the solar panel S is located precisely at the North Pole during the day of the Spring Equinox when the sun traces (approximately) along the curve.

$$\vec{F}(t) = \langle R \sin t, R \cos t, 0 \rangle$$

where R equals the distance between Earth and the sun, and $t \in [0, 2\pi]$ is the "time" of one revolution. The following integral expresses the accumulation of the sunbeam along panel S with the normal vector. $\vec{n}$:

$$\int_0^{2\pi} \left(\iint_D \vec{F}(t) \cdot \vec{n} \, dA \right) dt$$

Where D is the region of the parameters of the surface S such that $\vec{F}(t) \cdot \vec{n} > 0$. Here are sample assignments for the students:

A. Evaluate the accumulation along the horizontal panel, namely S is parameterized by $\{(x, y, 0): 0 \le x \le 1, 0 \le y \le 1\}$.

B. Evaluate the accumulation along the vertical panel, namely $\{(0, y, z): 0 \le y \le 1, 0 \le z \le 1\}$.

C. Evaluate the accumulation along the cylindrical panel described by the surface $r(u, v) = \langle \sin u, \cos u, v \rangle$ with $0 \le u \le 2\pi$ and $0 \le v \le 1$. If your result is 0, check the integration boundaries so that the condition $\vec{F}(t) \cdot \vec{n} > 0$ is satisfied.

Summarize your findings in a table. Given a square solar panel with area 1 made of a flexible medium, how would you shape it and locate it on the North Pole to maximize the sunbeam accumulation on the spring equinox day? Which shapes, in your opinion, are the most efficient in collecting the sunbeam? And why?

Figure. A spherical solar panel sample section for the North Pole.

Exercise: What always amazed me in this project was its beginning. Casual conversations with students can lead to a long-term project with multiple publications. Do you talk with your students? Do you know what topics they are interested in? What excites them, and what style of projects would they like to work on?

This project was modified multiple times, which led to publications with students. Here are several modifications to the initial project idea.

More projects about the geometry of solar panels can be found in (Marciniak & et al, 2017), (Pandya & et al, 2018), (Marciniak, Hassebo, & et al, Efficient geometry of flexible solar panels optimized for the latitude of New York City, 2018), (Cho & et al, 2019), (Chowdhury & Marciniak, 2019), (Chowdhury & et al, Optimization of solar cell packing models for flexible surfaces, 2020).

Title: Geometry of solar panels. Model for the Lunar Base

Math Topics: Curve parametrization, surface parametrization, surface integrals, etendue

Math Level: Calculus 3

The Sun's trajectory on the Moon's sky is much more complicated than the trajectory on the Earth. The motion of the sun on the moon's sky is subject to change in its speed and direction, which is created by the moon's libration, as described in (Maskal, Aboudiwan, & Marciniak, 2020; Maskal, Aboudiwan, & Marciniak, 2020). In this research, we create a

114

mathematical model of efficiency for geometrical solar panels based on the etendue, with the panel being the diaphragm and a selected segment of the sky being the source. The selected segment of the sky is crafted with an analysis of the moon's motion. A part of building the efficiency model is understanding the elliptical orbit of the Moon around the Sun, the Moon's ecliptic path, the latitudinal and longitudinal libration of the Moon, and the Moon's rotation about its axis. Efficiency is a holistic and cumulative value; it considers all potential moon orbit variations during its full lunar period. We analyze the luminosity on the moon to show that the difference between the perihelion and the aphelion on the moon's elliptic path can be omitted in our model. Luminosity also gives us a quantitative understanding of how much energy a solar panel at the lunar base can collect.

Etendue quantifies the relationship between a light source (surface S parameterized by $\vec{S}(\theta, \phi)$ with normal vector $\vec{N}$) and a light collector (diaphragm, surface r parameterized by $\vec{r}(x, y)$ with normal vector $\vec{n}$). To be precise, the etendue measures the agreement between the directions of the normal vectors ($\vec{N}$ and $\vec{n}$) from the two surfaces and is defined as a double surface integral of the dot product between two normal vectors:

$$Etendue = \iint_S \iint_r \vec{N} \cdot \vec{n} \, d\vec{r} \cdot d\vec{S}$$

In this model, the integration is performed only for the range of the parameters, where $\vec{N} \cdot \vec{n} > 0$. Calculating along the ranges of the parameters, where $\vec{N} \cdot \vec{n} < 0$ would indicate that the panel is losing energy when the sunlight shines on the non-photovoltaic side of the panel, which does not occur. In our model, the solar panel is the diaphragm, and a selected segment of the sky is the light source. The paper analyzes several shapes of the moon's Poles and the equator.

Figure. Equator. A sketch of the light source used in the etendue.

A full lunar period is known to be equal to 18.6 (Earth) years. In our model, we assume that over the full lunar period, a summation of each sinusoidal curve created by the Sun's path on the Moon's sky per lunar day is represented by a spherical segment and parameterized by:

$$\vec{S}(\theta, \phi) = \langle \cos\theta \sin\phi, \sin\theta \sin\phi, \cos\phi \rangle.$$

The coordinate system in this model is chosen the same way as in the previous models on Earth. The spherical segment represents the part of the sky where the sun will travel. This spherical segment is said to have a width represented by the maximum and minimum amplitude of ϕ. Thus, the parameters θ and ϕ have the following ranges:

On the North Pole: $\theta \in [0, 2\pi]$ and $\phi \in \left[\frac{\pi}{2} - 0.15, \frac{\pi}{2}\right]$

On the Equator: $\theta \in [-\frac{\pi}{2}, \frac{\pi}{2}]$ and $\phi \in \left[\frac{\pi}{2} - 0.15, \frac{\pi}{2} + 0.15\right]$

Assignment: Using parametrizations of various solar panel surfaces (in various positions), find their Etendue. Based on your calculations decide which surfaces produce more energy. How would you decide how to trim those surfaces to keep their efficiency high across the entire surface?

Title: Starting a Lunar Base

Math topics: Second order Linear equations

Math course: Differential Equations

This is a comprehensive project where students developed strategies for creating the entire lunar base. They asked, answered questions, and provided reasoning, analyzing multiple perspectives. The very first question was related to a suitable base location. Due to the limited amount of light and variability of temperatures, the location had to be carefully chosen. Students agreed that the base should be modular and placed on the Shackleton or Nova crater near deposits of ice. While analyzing the possibility of using solar panels to power the base, students realized that tracking systems should be avoided so as not to excite the lunar dust. After analyzing and discussing all the factors and pros and cons of the ideas, the team did not resolve the challenge of one problem: cleaning the dust from the stationary solar panels. Thus, this topic became a theme for the following research project. Over time, lunar dust would begin to cover the surface of the solar panels, reducing their efficiency in acquiring energy from the sun. Therefore, electrostatic and di-electrophoresis are viable ways to deal with this issue. Electrostatic would be the system in charge of removing electrically charged particles, while di-electrophoresis would remove particles not electrically charged by the solar wind. According to Kawamoto (Kawamoto & et al, 2011) motion of the dust can be moved along the panels (approximately) according to the following system of differential equations:

$$m_i \ddot{x}_i = -6\pi\mu R\dot{x} + q_i E + F_{image} + F_{dipole} + F_{adhesion} + m_i g$$

$$I_i \ddot{\theta}_i = 0$$

where the variables x and θ represent the different directions and angles at which the particles can move. Other variables, such as $m, g, \mu, R, q, I,$

refer to the mass of the particles, gravity, viscosity of air, radius of the particles, electric charges, and inertia, respectively.

Assignment: Imagine that the panels are 5in x 5in squares. Will the dust be moved away from the panels? If the panels are enlarged to 15in x 15 in, how will the change of size affect the time needed to clean the dust from the surface of the panels?

Exercise: Designing a lunar base creates numerous opportunities to make new problems. Will the base generate a sufficient amount of power? If it is built by robots, where do they rest and recharge? What rocks are under the moon's surface, and can they be shaped to create more underground tunnels? How hard are the rocks? In our imagination, we envisioned magnetic trains in the tunnels to move around between different bases.

We thought that augers could drill and pour concrete to build tunnels in lava. We designed our tools for working on the Moon. Ultimately, we decided to have expandable solar towers that fold at night in heated capsules.

Title: Agrivoltaics

Math topic: Angle of elevation

Math Level: Trigonometry

Agrivoltaics refers to using the power of solar panels in combination with crop growth. Plants can produce biomass with indirect sunlight using the space available beneath solar panels, while simultaneously the photovoltaic cells generate electricity. This is a harmonious relationship since solar panels allow plants to receive indirect sunlight.

Figure. Agrivoltaics

About 2715 Watts of electricity is needed to run our farm's drip irrigation system daily. Since conventional solar panels produce about 250 Watts every hour under ideal conditions, we would only need a few solar panels to power our irrigation system. This means that all excess energy can be fed into the grid, providing renewable energy for the community and creating additional income opportunities for the farmer.

Assignment: Design a 231–acre 119grivoltaics farm near the equator that runs its drip irrigation systems on renewable solar energy. The research can focus on optimizing the layout of the solar panels to maximize the farm's energy and food production.

For a sample layout, assume that the posts are 2 meters high, the panels are 2 meters long, and the distance between the rows is 2 meters. Check whether all plants underneath the panels have a sufficient amount of light. For example, basil needs 6-8 hours, while the length of day near the Equator is 12 hours.

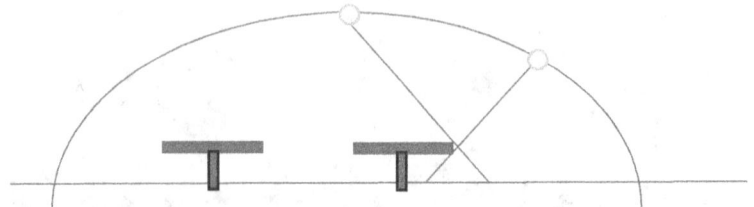

Figure. The position of the shade depends on the position of the sun

Exercise: This framework allows multiple questions, for example, given a particular plant, how the distance between the panels should be adjusted to allow a given number of hours of direct sunshine. How should the rows of panels be constructed to allow flexibility in the choice of plants?

More about agrivoltaics can be found in (Hassanpour, Slker, & Higgins, 2018)

Title: Floating solar panels

Math Topic: Angle of elevation, refraction,

Math Level: Trigonometry

Solar energy is one of the most significant renewable energy sources. Unfortunately, when the weather temperature is above 25 degrees Celsius, the solar panel power output is reduced by 10- 25%. This project compares the ground and roof-mounted solar panels to the floating solar panels. Floating solar panels have some advantages. The water-cooling effect on floating solar panels decreases their overheating and increases their efficiency by up to 20%. We save valuable land space by installing solar panels on bodies of water such as hydroelectric dam reservoirs, wastewater treatment ponds, or drinking water reservoirs. It has environmental benefits; the shade of solar panels reduces the evaporation of water. The transmission over long distances of electricity creates power

120

losses; 8-15% of electricity is lost between the power plant and consumers. It causes nearly a billion metric tons of carbon dioxide emissions into the atmosphere every year worldwide. The floating solar panels can be built safely close to the cities to minimize energy loss. West African countries, some states of the United States of America (Hawaii, Florida, Louisiana, Arizona, Texas, etc.,) and other countries that experience hot temperatures and dry climates are the best locations to mount the floating solar panels. As much as it seems advantageous from the perspective of exploitation of natural resources, the environmental impact must be simulated before the panels are installed on the water's surface. A simple model can be performed for locations near the equator.

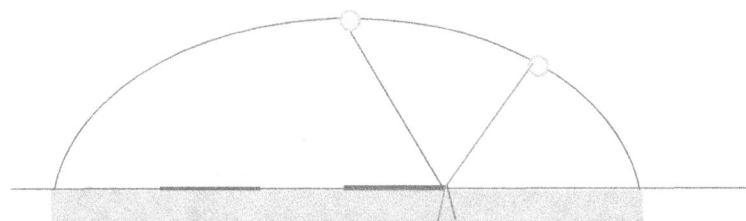

Figure. The shade inside the lake depends on the position of the sun.

Assuming that the refraction index is 1.33 and that water plants need about 8-10 hours of sunlight per day, design a distribution of solar panels on the surface of a lake. Should 1-meter-long panels be considered? Or 2-meter-long panels? How far apart should they be so every place underneath them has at least 8-10 hours of sunlight?

Exercise: This project is somehow a generalization of the previous project with the new component in the form of the index of refraction. What other

121

generalizations and their interpretations are readily available in this model?

More about floating photovoltaics can be found in (Majid, Ruslan, Sopian, Othman, & Azmi, 2014)

Computer Science

While searching for appealing scenarios for students' projects, I asked my students about what interests them. Students indicated they would use tracing programs, encryption, motherboard, and cost optimization of geothermal energy projects depending on the required drilling depth. A female student who chose a textbook project about the rainbow suggested that the project could be expanded into diffraction and reflections in other media, not only in the water droplets. In the future, I will keep preparing new assignments and collecting students' suggestions.

Title: priority switches

Math Topics: Differentiation, Integration

Math Level: Calculus 1, Calculus 2

After pairing a smartwatch with my cellphone, I noticed a significant drop in the quality of Zoom meetings. This reminded me of multiple complaints from students during remote classes when they claimed that their internet is excellent, but sometimes, due to unknown reasons, the quality is disturbed. It is possible that multiple devices connected to their computers (security cameras, doorbells, heaters, air conditioners, washers, dryers, water kettles, smartwatches, Bluetooth speakers, TVs, etc.) were competing. This assignment brings attention to this issue and is informative and educational.

Two devices or apps compete for communication on the smartphone (let us say, smartwatch and Zoom app). Their data is sent according to the functions $f_1(x) = \frac{1+\sin x}{2}$ and $f_2(x) = \frac{1+\sin(2x-\frac{\pi}{6})}{2}$, respectively. When the value of $f_1(x) + f_2(x)$ exceeds 1, which is 100% of the capacity of the devices that begin competing. The actual data transfer cannot exceed one; thus, the transfer follows the function $D(x) = \min\{1, (f_1 + f_2)(x)\}$.

The switch prioritizes the device with a larger derivative (sudden increment of data). If at a given time x, $(f_1 + f_2)(x) < 1$ then both signals are sent without interruption.

Assume that at a given time x, $(f_1 + f_2)(x) > 1$ then the following "switch" is applied:

-choose $f_1(x)$ if $f_1'(x) > f_2'(x)$,

-choose $f_2(x)$ if $f_2'(x) > f_1'(x)$.

Questions:

a) Use software to sketch the graph of the function $D(x) = \min\{1, (f_1 + f_2)(x)\}$ which models the data usage.

b) On the graph of $D(x)$ mark in red the intervals where the data from f_1 is transferred, and in blue where the data from f_2 is transferred.

c) Compare the priority of using the first device (smartwatch) to the second device (Zoom app). Do you think designing the priority this way will cause disruptions while using Zoom? Do you think that this will cause disruptions while using a smartwatch?

d) Describe the functions that model the delays on each device.

e) How would you modify this priority to better match the needs of the users?

Below is a sample graph of the functions $(f_1 + f_2)(x)$ and $D(x)$.

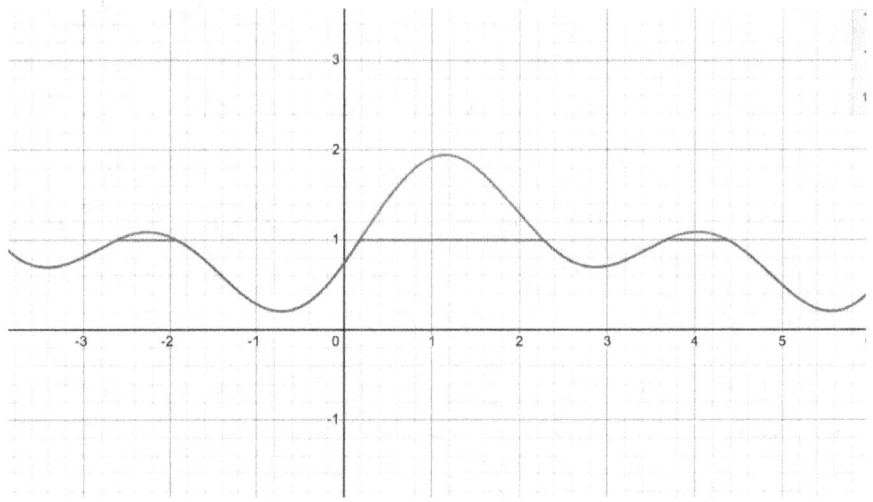

Figure. Graphs of the functions $(f_1 + f_2)(x)$ and $D(x)$.

Exercise: The priority switches can be defined in many ways, for example, with integrals, where the accumulation of information (not the sudden increment) changes the decision. Can you find other definitions of priority switches and provide suitable reasonings for them? Here are some examples with parameter α.

SWITCH 1 (additive)

-choose $f_1(x)$ if $f_1{'}(x) > f_2'(x) + α$,

-choose $f_2(x)$ otherwise

SWITCH 2 (multiplicative)

-choose $f_1(x)$ if $f_1{'}(x) > αf_2'(x)$,

-choose $f_2(x)$ otherwise

Determine the reasonable value of α for the functions $f_1(x)$ and $f_2(x)$ defined before.

Where would you search for the actual values of $f_1(x)$ and $f_2(x)$?

The Bull Transcended

Astride the Ox, I reach home.
I am serene. The Ox, too, can rest.
The dawn has come. In blissful repose,
Within my thatched dwelling
I have abandoned the whip and ropes.

—7—

Classroom

Once the habit of creative thinking is established, innovative ideas flow freely within any framework and at any level. However, being "live" in creativity may bring unexpected emotions, and their influence may be very positive, carrying the thought of "I need it now." Alternatively, others may experience sudden blockages of creative thought due to the immediate need or being watched.

When the connections between conscious and subconscious are established, the brief assignments in the classroom become natural. There is no need to assign them every day and for every topic. However, having a selection of such topics to use as needed is convenient.

Brief assignments

Here are a few samples of brief creative assignments for undergraduate courses. Introducing them in my classes brought a different light to the learning process, exposing the creative strengths of usually quiet students and the weaknesses of students who are very good at following directions but only within the usual learning paths.

Undoubtedly, there are vast possibilities for finding brief assignments and creative aspects that may be as diverse as the teachers worldwide. I aimed to design a creative assignment to initiate creative learning process in class. Further development of my creative skills led to refined assignments that addressed particular challenges in the course. However, the key was to initially incorporate as many brief creative assignments as possible, then refine and select the most valuable ones. The selection, however, is not set in stone and varies depending on the circumstances.

While reflecting on refining and assessing the brief creative assignments, I recall that the most valuable insightful moments took place in the classroom while observing students and their reactions. For example, in the differential equations course, I noticed students' confusion when, for the first time, they were exposed to a creative assignment. Most students did not know what to do and looked around to check what others were doing. Then, they waited to see what other students wrote on the board. However, most students began working immediately without hesitation during the second creative assignment. Yet still, some did not work, claiming they were not used to such assignments. Coincidentally, one of such students participated in a year-long project and proved to be a creative scholar who later continued his education to graduate levels.

Similar memorable moments of bliss happened in mathematics courses and during the freshman seminar meetings or lectures for a broad audience. For example, in the freshman seminar, I observed students' hesitation while choosing a partner for a discussion. As a result, I decided to assign groups on my own rather than allow students to have a free choice. Another critical observation happened during a lecture about the Spirograph when students were asked whether or under what circumstances the drawing curve can reach the point where it started. One student responded that such a curve always has such property and justified his opinion in a way that opened my eyes to a different way of thinking. The student said he did not find one to continue infinitely while drawing curves with the spirograph. Thus, he concluded that all epicycloids must end at the same point where they began. This way of thinking is undoubtedly incorrect, but without hearing it from a student, I would not even think of that alone.

Writing and understanding definitions of limits in Calculus 1

Creative teachers have a capacity for immediate and effortless adjustments to new circumstances. Below is an example of a transformation of a brief creative class assignment from Calculus 1 that accommodates writing and possibly an AI chatbot.

In a Calculus 1 classroom, discussion about limits begins with ideas and graphs, and at some point, the teacher introduces a formal definition of a limit. The definition of a finite limit is different than the infinite limit. Similarly, a definition at a finite point differs from that at infinity. The teacher shows the students these three definitions and examples and then asks the students to write a formal definition of the infinite limit at infinity. Students perform the assignment on their own and then check in groups with one another for errors and understanding. A modified version of this assignment involves a chatbot. Here, students compare their work with a definition created by a chatbot for accuracy and understanding.

This assignment can be used in class to help understand definitions of limits and it can also be assigned as homework or quiz problem. If given as a graded assignment, partial credit should be awarded generously accompanied by a detailed feedback and a follow-up discussion to address any potential gaps in student understanding.

Providing examples of linear and non-linear differential equations.

During the first meeting of the Differential Equations course, one can introduce a brief creative assignment where students, after learning the definition of linear differential equations, create their examples of linear and nonlinear differential equations. They would also describe why, in their opinion, the equations have that particular property. Some students get confused or simply imitate examples provided on the board and experience difficulties creating unique ideas of nonlinear equations. However, after seeing creative examples from other students, they got accustomed to the idea of a creative class environment and began enjoying the activity.

Exercise: You can undoubtedly pick a course you teach and find a suitable place to introduce similar "examples creating" assignments. However, it may be more productive to think the other way around and search for definitions of mathematical objects that create an excellent space for wandering about possible examples and counterexamples. Then, see which courses you teach may accommodate these definitions.

Justifying mathematical convention in Calculus 3 class

Often, Calculus 3 students have difficulties understanding why the 3-dimensional space is represented with the yz-plane being drawn as the plane of the board or paper and the $x - axis$ coming out of the board with the positive direction pointing towards the observer. To address this issue, I introduced a brief creative assignment, where each student made a few sketches with suggestions on how the three-dimensional space could be drawn. Then, students presented their work on the board and plotted the point (1,2,3). When the pictures were compared, it became evident that prior to understanding each other's drawings at first glance, we had to stay within one convention. At the same time, students recognized positive and negative-oriented 3-dimensional spaces. Group work is handy for this activity since students can look at each other's drawings to compare and verify whether two pictures represent the same 3-dimensional space or its mirror image. The activity took about 15 minutes of class time.

Exercise: This is a watered-down version of the previous assignment since it does not involve mathematical definitions but only the notation. However, such assignments may be helpful in highly diverse classrooms with students with experience in various educational systems. To find a good topic, such as an assignment that would fit your courses, simply think of a topic where students display diverse styles, preventing them from comparing the answers.

Justifying mathematical terminology in Linear Algebra

Usually, the terminology of math concepts reflects on their connections with life examples, the name of a person honored, or simply another idea. The general motivation for providing appropriate math terminology is to connect the concept and vocabulary. However, those ideas may sometimes be so particular and exquisite that modern education does not give students the necessary knowledge to make this connection. In such a case, math terminology may become an actual burden unless it is used as an excuse to expose students to new topics. The echelon form of a matrix is an example of a perfectly placed similarity between the appearance of a reduced matrix and military formations known already in Roman times. A brief creative assignment involves students searching on their cell phones for answers to questions about the right and left echelon forms and their relationship to matrices. Students are asked to prepare a brief description of what "echelon" means and should visualize their presentation with a picture or a photo. The activity can be performed in class or assigned as homework.

Exercise: This assignment is significant for bilingual students and instructors. To find suitable terminology for clarification, one can

Providing real-life examples in Calculus 3 class

Frequently, mathematics teachers receive requests from students to clearly state the life applications of presented methods, concepts, and theorems. The classroom approach to such an inquiry involves asking students what examples they can provide based on their experience. When introducing quadric surfaces and parametric curves, my students spend time in the classroom finding familiar shapes similar to those on the screen. Usually, the examples are divided into those that appear in nature and those that are man-made. The most frequently analyzed curves are the helix and the spiral. When looking at them, students recall car shocks, springs inside pens, or side-spiral college notebooks. Students often claim that there is only one spiral while analyzing the physical models of the spirals; it just needs to be "turned around." However, after rotating the model several times, they eventually arrive at the illuminating conclusion that the two spirals are not identical.

Among the surfaces, the saddle is the most difficult to sketch but provides the most satisfying examples in the form of Pringles potato chips. When sketching the shape of a paraboloid $z = 8 - x^2 - y^2$ trimmed to the region $-1 \le x \le 1, 0 \le y \le 2$, a student realized that the graph reminded him of a parachute segment.

Similarly, we sketched a picture of the solid outside the cylinder when introducing triple integrals in cylindrical and spherical coordinates. $x^2 + y^2 = 1$ and inside the sphere $x^2 + y^2 + z^2 = 4$. When looking at this solid, students were asked what real-life shapes come to mind. Students pointed out that some beads are shaped just like solids.

Exercise: Calculus 3 is a course where many students seriously struggle while making attempts to connect their mathematics skills with spatial vision. If you teach geometry, you can undoubtedly find applications that resemble given geometrical shapes. However, maybe this is an excellent place to go one step beyond the provided example and search for topics in your courses that require students to build connections between their math skills and some other skills (this could be reading while working on word problems). What creative assignments could students perform to improve such connections?

Exercise: Going one step beyond the previous idea, one can ask for the existing objects composed of two or more quadric surfaces. This requires three-dimensional surgery and gluing.

Exercise inspired by (Weisberg & Reeves, 2013): *Invent applications for imaginary objects that are compositions of two or more quadric surfaces. Give them names, practical materials, and appealing colors.*

Providing mathematical examples of typical regions in Calculus 3

In the past, before I committed to introducing creative assignments in my classes, I prepared a neatly organized sequence of examples to introduce students to a variety of typical regions. Then, I presented those examples in class and asked students to describe the boundaries of the regions. When my perspective changed, the definition was followed by one example, and then I asked students to produce their examples. After receiving my feedback and encouragement, students worked on the assignment for about 15 minutes and presented their work on the board. While observing the class, I realized that some students immediately began producing examples, but some had no trust in their minds and simply did not know what region to think of. I directed those students to the recent worksheet with an example of a domain of a function. As I observed, most students who began working promptly started with a region in their mind and then tried to obtain functions that matched the shape of their example. After reviewing many students' examples, I realized the variety was just as good as in the lecture I prepared. At the end of the activity, students sketched their regions on the board and provided their solutions. Then, I analyzed all the solutions and corrected the mistakes on the board. Students seemed more interested and involved in the topic than usual.

Exercise: This is an example of co-creating the flow of the class together with students. It may be wise to choose a relatively easy topic at the beginning and later try something more challenging. What easy topics would you choose for such a class design? What would be the second selection of slightly more complex topics? How would you alter the method of co-creative flow to suit your teaching style and students' needs?

Entertaining historical remarks

The student body in my Differential Equations and Calculus 3 classes consists mainly of engineering students. Knowing how serious they are in their studies, I was very skeptical whether they even would be interested in the historical backgrounds and biographies of mathematicians. However, my students seemed to be very interested and involved in discussions. At the end of the semester, we introduce the Laplace transform. To make the topic more "human," I mention the biography of Laplace and briefly discuss different integral transformations that were known in his times. I have realized that students favor odd and silly things that mathematicians do or say. For example, while talking about Laplace, they laugh when I disclose that in his book "Theorie Analytique Probabilities," he did not give credit to his precursors (Laplace, 1812). Providing no references to research done by other authors was already considered bad manners in the 18th century.

Inquiries about terminology and a mathematician in Differential Equations

This example of a brief creative classroom assignment has its roots in the epistemological remarks related to the mysterious name of the Wronskian. To explain the origin of the name, one needs to mention a Polish mathematician and philosopher, Józef Maria Hoëné-Wroński. Students very much enjoyed the fact that Wroński did not receive much recognition during his life, and his work was dismissed as rubbish. However, he was the one who introduced the expansion of a function into a series. Hoëné-Wroński was considered a phony, and his philosophical ideas about Polish Messianism were dismissed entirely. My students particularly appreciate people who lived "out of the grid" because they often feel unaccomplished and underrated, working low-paid jobs as drivers, bartenders, or handymen while simultaneously studying to be engineers.

Even without lengthy and laborious preparations, an instructor can simply open a Wikipedia page and ask students what questions they have about the life accomplishments of the person behind specific terminology, convention, or a theorem. My students asked how Hoëné-Wroński could be at the same time a philosopher, mathematician, physicist, inventor, lawyer, occultist, and economist. Then we discussed that education was shaped differently on the edge of the eighteenth and nineteenth centuries since the sciences were not as developed and students had to study much less. An excellent collection of anecdotes and historical remarks can be found in "Differential Equations with Applications and Historical Notes" by George F. Simmons (Simmons, 2018).

Exercise: Which mathematicians feel inspiring, and which would you like to display in your classes? Are their works present in the courses that you teach? If not, then what are other reasons you could display their biography?

I continually wondered how to evaluate the presence of historical and epistemological remarks in a classroom. Then I realized that students repeat what they value, and finding such remarks in the students' class projects proves their interest and involvement.

Observations and Challenges

While observing students during their creative work, I realized that some did not get involved with the question and did not experience the illumination stage. However, I would still consider the assignment successful from the perspective of those students since they were somehow exposed to the process when observing their peers going through all four stages of creativity. Moreover, the process was repeated multiple times in the classroom, and thus the observations were recurrent. I hope that during those brief assignments, the classroom offered a safe and friendly environment for students to encourage and practice the habit of creativity while learning the material. Some students experienced the illumination stage, visible even from a distance through a facial expression or a subtle jump of energy within the body.

As a teacher and a mentor of multiple research projects, I have been searching for methods of gently tapping into students' subconscious minds to reveal the hidden potential of creativity. I believe that the habit of creativity can be trained just like other habits of mind. However, the training requires a suitable environment and appropriate circumstances to produce creative illumination.

Conclusions

Students' involvement, reactions to the brief creative assignments, and the survey results indicate that this class activity is joyfully welcomed in the classroom. However, the most crucial benefit of creative assignments is binding the conscious and subconscious mind by creating an everlasting conversation among their mental formations. Those conversations may seem insignificant to the entire course curriculum and marginal from the perspective of learning calculus, but they are essential or crucial for the unity of knowledge.

Exercise: Brief creative assignments are a mid-step towards long creative assignments, but at this stage, observing the classroom carefully and your reactions is crucial. Students are susceptible to the instructor's nonverbal feedback, especially regarding personal judgment. What observations did you make during the brief creative assignments? Did you try various types and various courses? Type up notes from all occurrences and seek patterns.

Long assignments

From the first day of the semester, students are exposed to the idea of doing something new and creative. They go through brief creative assignments, receive feedback on their writing, discuss their solutions in front of an audience, and get to know their classmates during group work. In the long creative projects, all the skills that students practiced in class come together. I provide samples of students' work from previous semesters to give new students a taste of such long creative projects. In the past, I presented some aspects of these projects with old PowerPoint slides. However, starting in the spring of 2019, I began using fragments of videos taken previously during students' presentations (with their permission). In my understanding, seeing enthusiastic students presenting their projects is a form of positive encouragement to engage in a similar activity. Recently, during the pandemic when all classes were in a remote modality, instead of life presentations in the classroom, students submitted their work as a video presentation.

In all courses, students can work on a "standard" topic using their selection of creative elements. Alternatively, they can work on a "nonstandard" topic.

Another option is to invent a new topic, which is chosen by students frequently enough to keep such an option. At the same time, students can work on their own or in a group. I hope that this variety of options accommodates the needs of diverse student groups.

Here are several examples of creative aspects of students' work for the final classroom projects.

Linear Algebra Project 3-D Transformations.

A computer science student brought his way of presenting 3-dimensional transformations with matrices using Excel. Here is the student's work (after a minor makeover):

Basic rotations in 3D space are different than in 2D space. In 3D space, an object can rotate with respect to the x, y, and z-axis. So, rotations in 3D space have three rotation matrices.

$$M_{rx} = \begin{bmatrix} 1 & 0 & 0 \\ 0 & \cos\theta & -\sin\theta \\ 0 & \sin\theta & \cos\theta \end{bmatrix}$$

$$M_{ry} = \begin{bmatrix} \cos\theta & 0 & \sin\theta \\ 0 & 1 & 0 \\ -\sin\theta & 0 & \cos\theta \end{bmatrix}$$

$$M_{rz} = \begin{bmatrix} \cos\theta & -\sin\theta & 0 \\ \sin\theta & \cos\theta & 0 \\ 0 & 0 & 1 \end{bmatrix}$$

$$M_t = M_{rx} \times M_{ry} \times M_{rz} \times M_0$$

$$= \begin{bmatrix} 1 & 0 & 0 \\ 0 & cos45° & -sin45° \\ 0 & sin45° & cos45° \end{bmatrix} \times \begin{bmatrix} cos45° & 0 & sin45° \\ 0 & 1 & 0 \\ -sin45° & 0 & cos45° \end{bmatrix} \times$$

$$\begin{bmatrix} cos45° & -sin45° & 0 \\ sin45° & cos\theta45° & 0 \\ 0 & 0 & 1 \end{bmatrix} \times \begin{bmatrix} 0 & 5 & 0 & 0 \\ 0 & 0 & 5 & 0 \\ 0 & 0 & 0 & 5 \end{bmatrix} =$$

$$\begin{bmatrix} 0 & 2.5 & -.732 & 4.268 \\ 0 & 2.5 & 4.268 & -0.732 \\ 0 & -3.536 & 2.5 & 2.5 \end{bmatrix}$$

I did not realize what was creative about the student's work until another computer science student asked how the program was written since Excel does not support 3-dimensional pictures. Then, the author opened another file and explained that he projected 3-dimensional pictures on 2-dimensional planes using matrices. I thought this was a creative way of using linear transformations and Excel programming.

Calculus 3 Project Escape Velocity.

After presenting his assignment, the student presented a slide entitled "Bonus!" He asked the following question: What is the minimum velocity an object needs to escape the gravitational pull of an average human body? Assume that the average human mass is $M = 70kg$, the average human density is $\varrho = 985 \, kg/m^3$. Moreover, humans are shaped as spheres.

Using equations $Vol_{sphere} = \frac{4\pi r^3}{3}$ and $Vol = \frac{M}{\varrho}$, found $r = 0.257$ and

$$v = \sqrt{\frac{2GM}{r}}$$

Plug $r = 0.257$ m, $G = 6.67 * 10^{-11} Nm^2 kg^{-2}$ and $M = 70kg$ to obtain

$$v = \sqrt{\frac{2 * 6.67 * 10^{-11} * 70}{0.257}} = 1.91 * 10^{-4} m/s = 191 \ micrometers/second$$

At the end of this presentation, all students discussed what objects move with such a speed.

Pendulum wave.

One of my students described his creative flow while working on a class assignment. His Differential Equations project was about a simple pendulum. However, he wanted to show an experiment to illustrate the formula that expresses the dependence between the string length and the pendulum's period. He found an experiment called pendulum wave online and decided to build a wooden frame and present the experiment in class. Here is his description of his process of searching and building the model (Delshad, 2018):

"Recently, I built a pendulum wave. A pendulum wave is a structure based on a series of pendulums in a row, with equal distance apart from each other. Each pendulum in that series has a different length, so lengths are calculated with precise accuracy using a formula. This difference in the length of the pendulums creates different periods for every pendulum in the series. This effect causes the pendulum wave to create patterns like moving waves, helixes, chaotic motion, etc.

I saw someone build a pendulum wave structure online, which was mesmerizing. Now, I wanted to create my pendulum wave. Also, I wanted to understand the laws of physics, such as kinetic energy, potential energy, the motion of a wave, and the characteristics of this pendulum wave. First, I understood the concepts as much as I could on a piece of paper. I understood that the summation of kinetic and potential energy equals zero. It was easy to comprehend that energy cannot be created or destroyed.

$P.E = mgh$ $\qquad\qquad\qquad K.E = \frac{1}{2}mv^2$

P.E + K.E = 0

Time period of a pendulum = $2\pi\sqrt{\dfrac{l}{g}}$ where l is length and g is gravitational acceleration

The process of building the pendulum wave was full of happy and challenging moments. There were a couple of stages that needed to be accomplished. I will go through all the stages one by one. First of all, I sketched the pendulum wave structure on a piece of paper. I choose to have 12 pendulums in my series. From the research, I knew I had to choose the length of the first pendulum and T_{max} for the wave. Where T_{max} is the period of the pendulum wave. Using the formula below, I calculated the length of each pendulum and accurately noted it on the piece of paper. This formula is derived from the formula above (1) with an additional constant k.

$$L\ (n) = g\left[\left[\frac{T_{max}}{2\pi(k+n+1)}\right]\right]^2$$

g = gravitational acceleration T_{max} *= Time period of the pendulum wave*

k = constant   *n = number of pendulum in the series*

To find out the value of the constant k, I plugged in T_{max} as 24 seconds, g, first length = 0.254 meters, n = 1 (first pendulum), and solved for k. Whatever the k value I got, it stays the same for the entire project. So, I wrote a C++ program that helped me easily calculate the length of all the pendulums in the series. After learning the lengths of every pendulum in the series, I noted all the materials needed to build a pendulum wave.

Since I knew that my pendulum weights were 0.5 cm (centimeters) wide, I kept all the pendulums 1.5 cm apart so they would not be tangled up.

This part of the project can be understood easily because if I kept the pendulums too close, they would collide, and all the pendulums would get tangled up.

When I was building the pendulum wave, there were difficulties like setting pendulums in the series too close to each other, and they would get tangled up, or I would set up the pendulums in the series too far from each other, and this would make it difficult to swing all pendulums at the same time. Both situations had to be overcome by adjusting the distance between the pendulums. An important note is to keep the distance from one another pendulum the same for the entire series. One way to know if you have set up the pendulum's proper distance apart from each other is that the pendulum string does not get tangled up with another one. The proper separation also depends on your hanging weight. It is always better to have the right tools for the right job. Before starting any project, one should have all the necessary material to the best of their knowledge. If something else is needed later during the project, it can be acquired, and it is fine, but having all the necessary items before starting the project will put you in a better position to build. Last but not least, when building any projects, one should consider the budget and build accordingly."

In this example, the student's work was not original, but he was creative while figuring out what experiment he could show for his project. Then, while building the frame, he had difficulties with entangled strings and had to overcome this issue. The last aspect is more of a practical problem, but since the student is earning his engineering degree, this may be the kind of problem that he will be working on.

Differential Equations Project Simple Pendulum 2

The assignment was identical to the one described in the previous example, but students' input unfolded in another direction. Instead of bringing an experiment to visualize the topic, they brought a historical background and motivations to their presentation. They mentioned a pendulum clock and divination used for witchcraft, finding water, and gaining information. Such a selection may seem unusual for a team of engineers, but the class reacted positively.

Sculpture calculations

This assignment combines mathematical and non-mathematical ways of reflecting on a sculpture. Students present their work to the entire class using PowerPoint slides.

Figure. The sculpture used for the project.

Our college owns a sculpture by Isamu Noguchi (https://en.wikipedia.org/wiki/Isamu_Noguchi) located in the courtyard. Look at the sculpture and try to answer the following subjective and objective questions:

- Do you like this sculpture?

- What does the sculpture remind you of?

- Would you imagine "redoing" the sculpture on your own to make it more appealing? What would you do?

- Using methods from physics and mathematics, calculate the following mathematical features of the sculpture: the surface area (to approximate how much paint is needed), the volume and the mass (using average metal density), the center of mass (if it needs to be moved to another location)

- Explain your way of thinking when presenting your calculations.

- In your submission, show the sculpture's photo and possible re-design suggestions.

Finding topics

Recently, I experienced creativity very clearly while speaking with a student about possible project topics. I intended to find a topic that interests him, and that fits my capacity. Usually, I start such a conversation by asking the student about his interests and hobbies, and this particular student was, in the past, a firefighter. This made me think about my previous projects in the new circumstances of firefighting. My projects are about solar panels and aerodynamics, and since I could not think of solar panels being in a fire and still functioning, I focused on aerodynamics. In the aerodynamics project, we work on optimizing the design of the parameters of the blades of a wind turbine. I kept thinking about the fire and the wings of wind turbines, and then suddenly, I visualized drones flying into the fire and replacing the firefighters in the dangerous part of their work. That was my concept, but we did not simply end there. In the second stage of the discussion, I asked the student what functions he saw for drones. He thought for a few seconds and mentioned the situation when the firetruck could not arrive at the scene because of traffic. I was thinking about a friend's situation, her car catching on fire, her fear, and lack of help. This would be a situation where drones can patrol a highway and provide immediate response during accidents and situations that require help. I asked my students to think of the different functions of the drones and different designs they would need. However, I was thinking of combining the functions of the thermal camera and the drones to search for a fire in a city. When I looked at my student, I observed the light that filled him when he thought of working on such a project. We both agreed that our conversation was very fruitful and made our day.

Exercise: Finding or designing experiments that visualize some aspects of existing projects may be engaging, especially for engineering students. Which of the existing assignments could accommodate an available experiment to your students? At the same time, basic programming may engage computer science students. Which of the existing projects could accommodate programming aspects?

Alignment along creative assignments

Project topics are usually provided in the middle of the semester during the sixth week of classes. However, they are introduced in the syllabus and discussed during the first day of classes. Projects are worth 50 points out of 600 available in the course (one test is worth 100 points, the final exam is worth 200 points). Students are encouraged to search for project topics that align with their hobbies, interests, and majors, but sample topics are provided.

Students have a choice of working in small groups or individually. Since many students mentioned previous negative experiences while working in a group, I introduced self-assessment of crucial project skills such as writing, public speaking, math skills, and collaboration skills. All class activities aim to help students recognize the levels of their own and their colleagues' skills. While introducing the project guidelines, I point out that having all skills at the highest levels is a rarity; thus, students should focus on composing groups with their peers who possess complementary skills.

Writing

Throughout the semester, students submit two written paragraphs, the first of which is usually very short and consists of an explanation of how to perform a simple mathematical task. For example, in Calculus 3, students explain with simple language and in a few sentences how to plot the points (1,2,3) on the 3-dimensional coordinate system. The paragraphs are submitted as a thread to a discussion on Blackboard and read by me. I provide suggestions for corrections and request resubmissions if the paragraphs do not fulfill the directions from the rubrics. Students can see each other's work and check the writing skills of their colleagues. All tests and some quizzes contain written questions that ask them to describe step by step how to perform the solution of a given problem. I chose the problem in the past, but students suggested they would prefer to make their own choices. Thus, I will now provide a list of exam problems to choose from so that I can write a complete description. Following suggestions provided by faculty from the English Department, I suggest that students keep a reader in mind while writing. This reader is another student from their class who missed the topic they are describing.

Reading written samples from students has additional benefits. It helped me find in class those students who completely missed the point of a new lesson or did not understand some previous topics.

Communication and public speaking

In general, students fear public speaking and avoid it. Since solving problems on the board generates anxiety similar to public speaking, students often despise it. Again, motivated by students' suggestions, I introduced credit points for solving problems on the board and for finding mistakes that appeared there. Students can observe one another during those mini-presentations and, according to their judgment, place their public speaking skills within a group of peers. In addition to the common issues, many students in my classes are non-native English speakers, making public presentations even more challenging. However, for motivation, I emphasize that professional life carries equal challenges, and practicing public speaking at college may ease fears in the future.

Math skills

In all classes, the range of students' math skills may be broad, potentially preventing some individuals from completing the projects. Alternatively, some students may spend much time preparing their presentations to avoid spectacular failure in front of the entire class. Thus, students are encouraged to observe and be aware of their mathematical skill levels in class. As a teacher, I can support this awareness by providing information about students' positions among their peers. This information is required when students work in groups on test corrections after receiving their tests. Each group must have an identified student-leader who received a high score on the test. This prevents situations when students follow the loudest person in their team rather than focus on listening to the identified student-leader with the best score.

It has been a clear conclusion from research performed on college students that females tend to underestimate the ranking of their grades in class (Bloodhart & Balgopal, 2020). Hopefully, providing information on the actual ranking positively influences the graduation and retention of female students in engineering and computer science programs.

Collaboration skills

This skill set is probably neglected in math classes, but students benefit significantly if the teamwork is organized carefully, as described and reviewed (Ford, 2018). In my classes, teamwork is encouraged from the first day of classes when students meet each other during an ice-breaking activity. With a script, they form groups according to random signs on their copy and discuss their majors, ethnicity, hobbies, things they did over the weekend, etc. These scripted conversations often become loud laughs, and students form class teams based on those random arrangements. The most successful team-building activity happened in one of my classes when students remained in their original groups for the entire semester and refused to restructure. They learned their names, formed bonds, exchanged phone numbers, and met outside the classroom.

Throughout the semester, students have multiple chances to work with each other on various assignments. One of them, already mentioned above, allows students to work on their test corrections. After grading the tests and returning them to students, I promise students a few extra credit points for correcting errors. Students come to my office to explain their mistakes on the test and provide corrected solutions. Usually, I ask additional questions and furnish necessary clarifications. Another opportunity for students to work with their peers happens while completing the worksheets. Most lectures are accompanied by worksheets that consist of several sample problems. Usually, students work on one of them in class, and the remaining part is left as homework. I collect them regularly, grade them for correctness and completeness, and return them to students for corrections. Students submit all corrected and completed worksheets before the hour tests, often leaving this task for the last minute. Providing 30 minutes of class time for students to check their answers with each other saves me time. It also saves students time for future corrections and resubmissions.

Exercise: Your students may need a different set of skills to be successful in their future jobs. What are these skills? Do they practice these skills in your classroom? Would it be possible to incorporate the skills in the existing assignments?

Creativity is not listed among the skills that students assess and consciously develop during class. Moreover, there are some reasons why bringing students' consciousness to that topic is disputable. Csikszentmihalyi suggested in [1] that young researchers may not benefit from awareness of their creative process since excess of this insight may distract them from performing the creative thought. Nevertheless, some students may benefit from writing about their thinking while performing creative tasks.

Benefits of students' projects

I noted that attendance was maintained better when students presented their projects. In a personal conversation, students report that class material becomes blurry after a few semesters, but their and friends' presentations remain vivid for a long time.

Students expressed that they value group work and presentations since they resemble their workplace style, where multiple people collaborate, focus on the same task, and communicate their findings with the managers.

Challenges

Managing various topics and organizing presentations for multiple teams may be challenging in large classes. Sometimes, students request a change of topic or a group, which may bring some disorganization. Those problems may be related to students' tight schedules and difficulties scheduling meetings outside the class. Similarly, ambitious students may choose challenging topics and find out later in the semester that they do not have enough time to finish work on time.

Students arrived late and missed their presentations, pressing the instructor to organize additional meetings to accommodate their presentations outside the regular class schedule.

The most disturbing thing for the teacher may be the uneven level of presentations, where some students prepare lousy slides, mumble, and may show a lack of enthusiasm during the presentation. In contrast, others prepare well, wear suits and ties, and explain every detail of their work.

Assigning proper grades to each student for projects based on teamwork remains an unresolved question. So far, all students in a team have been awarded the same number of points. However, after being exposed to the works of (Ford, 2018), I have an intention of introducing individualized grading that involves students' reports about each other.

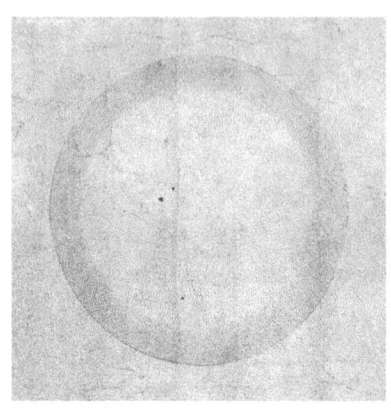

Both Bull and Self Transcended

Whip, rope, person, and Ox -
all merge in No Thing.
This heaven is so vast,
no message can stain it.
How may a snowflake exist
in a raging fire.
Here are the footprints of
the Ancestors.

—8—

Assessment

Specific measures can be used to assess growth when discussing the facilitation of creative skills. The Torrance Test of Creative Thinking is used as a formal assessment but may not always fit every classroom's scope. On the other hand, an informal assessment may help check the growth of creative skills or the quality of facilitation. Judging the final product based on reflections about the creation process would be rare for the industry. However, for self-assessment and educational purposes, the situation is not comparable to the free market. Here, the awareness of the process is the center of the attention. During the informal assessment proctored immediately after the brief creative assignment, I asked students whether they would prefer less or more of those assignments. Students agreed that wish for more since they found this activity valuable and encouraging.

Let us discuss a few ways of assessing creativity in education.

Agreeing on creative assignments

This aspect of creative activities may seem irrelevant to some instructors. However, in my understanding, students may not always feel comfortable trying to be creative without explicit consent to do creative assignments. To receive such clear yet informal statements from students, I usually mention the importance of creativity for their future and the lack of it in the college curriculum. Then, I ask whether students would like to try one creative assignment, even if it may feel weird. Once students agree to experiment, we try one brief creative problem. Collecting students' feedback and watching every aspect of their behavior, work, and state of mind is essential. Students' attitudes already differ during the second assignment, and they usually work on the second brief creative assignment more comfortably. The change between the second and the third assignment is not as spectacular. At the end of the semester, students react enthusiastically to creative ideas presented by their peers and receive congratulations. At that time students highly and explicitly appreciate creativity.

The reason for that approach from my side is the previous experiences of students' initial resistance to creative assignments. One of my students explained his discomfort, saying that he had never done anything like this before and was not expecting it; thus, the assignments initially confused him and stressed him incredibly. The same student complained about other assignments that did not fit within the standard classroom frames and went beyond common lecturing, homework, or quizzes. Amazingly, after working on a few creative assignments, the same student expressed his sincere interest in joining one of my research projects, knowing that the expectations go way beyond regular coursework. This student was exceptionally successful in working on open-ended questions. Later, he had a very successful education path and completed his master's degree (in computer science). In his appreciation letter, he mentioned that creative assignments changed him. I wish that all students have a chance to transform their minds through creative work.

Correctness and accuracy of creative ideas

When approaching a final product of someone else's creative work, we usually judge it by its quality, accuracy, usefulness or need, price on the market, rarity, or general appearance. This assessment of creative thought may seem the most obvious and the most suitable, but from the education perspective, it is simply too coarse for the subtleties of a growing mindset. Especially if "correctness" leads to discarding intermediate ideas that require refinement. Brief creative assignments at the early stages may confuse students, and they may not understand the question correctly. This assessment should be avoided at the early stages of the growth of creative thought.

The number of creative ideas

However, the ease of creating new ideas and a lack of attachment to existing ideas can measure the growth of creativity. During a brief creative assignment, students invent examples of non-linear differential equations, but some write nothing in their notes. After additional explanations and encouragement from the instructor, students provided examples that were bare imitations of those examples already written on the board. This displayed attachment toward the existing and known examples without placing them in a bigger context. Only one student was sufficiently brave to write down a "crazy" equation that did not resemble anything from the board. However, regardless of the instructor's encouragement, this student felt shy while sharing his example with the entire class. This story leads to another informal assessment of the improvement of creative thought.

Easiness of sharing new creative ideas

If students (and the instructor) fear appearing silly while sharing their initial, imperfect ideas, it will be difficult for the group to discuss and improve them. One of the possible measurements of mental growth is the capacity to share "working ideas" that are not entirely ready but can serve as a base for new discussions. This is particularly important in group assignments, where students must collaborate without fear. Only the insight into the creative thought process allows us to see the imperfect ideas as seeds for fruitful conversations.

Exercise: Do you share your creative ideas with ease? Or are you shy? How afraid are you to share your imperfect ideas with your students or colleagues? How afraid are you to make a mistake?

Frequency of spontaneous creative ideas

Any moment can carry creative ideas. Some people may have small creative ideas several times per day while taking care of daily chores, while at work, or while shopping for groceries. When observing students working on specific problems in the classroom, I often checked their collective distribution of ideas. Did most ideas happen at the beginning or the end of the session? Did ideas come in series? Or were the ideas certain "rarities" within the noise of incoherent thoughts? While observing group work, I had the impression that a series of ideas was not uncommon, which suggested some coordination within the group. When self-reflecting on the growth of my creative thoughts, I realized that creative work and reflections increased the frequency of creative ideas daily. However, ideas may not come when requested but appear during leisure time. Thus, following this observation, I consciously scheduled generous breaks in my work time, taking "a moment" for coffee or a simple look through the window. However, my best ideas still come in the shower, maybe due to the relaxation caused by warm water.

Diversity of ideas

Diversity of ideas measures how much the concepts spread within specific topics. For self-growth, one can observe creative ideas while working on a hobby but not at work or vice versa. As a teenager, I could write music and poems effortlessly and thus wanted to write songs, but music and words never came together. Thinking about a similar example in mathematical thinking, I could discuss the formalism and the intuition of proofs. Do they always come together or separately? I recall that I often had an intuition for proof but could not find the proper formalism to comprehend it. This state could take months or years before formal proof was revealed.

The lack of diversity of ideas may be related to specific attachments or the inability to forget certain paths of solutions. While searching for new solutions or ideas, this attachment may cause difficulty. It may be challenging to "forget" a particular way of thinking. Ample time taken for the Incubation stage may result from a long process of forgetting the existing solutions.

In the classroom, while assessing the growth of diversity of ideas, one can think about individual students or the entire group. While any assessment of the individuals may be quite challenging due to certain seldomness of creative thoughts, the group assessment always brings some observations.

Bravery while posing problems

Bravery may increase not only in the matter of having faith in your ideas but in having faith in posing problems and then possibly solving them. Posing problems are not always related to a particular portion of the material but may be related to challenging one's understanding. After introducing creative assignments in my classes, I realized that the atmosphere significantly improved, and students became more prompt to express doubts about their understanding of the material freely. Overall, this led to better understanding since every student received personalized explanations of the questions they asked. Creative spirit influenced learning spirit in the classroom bloomed after introducing creative assignments. Overall, this helped students improve their self-esteem while expressing their doubts and certainties about their understanding. Trust in one's thought process and problem-solving skills can help one attempt to solve more challenging problems.

Feeling easy about mistakes

One of the most unique and surprising results of getting more creative in my life was a change in my reactions to my own and other mistakes. In particular, my students no longer feel penalized for making mistakes since, in my words, actions, and attitudes, I have been convincing them that knowing their mistakes is a necessary stage of learning. Roughly speaking, two mindful individuals retain about 80% of a conversation. Their minds simply patch the remaining part with some errors. These errors remain hidden without a feedback loop where they can verify their understanding. In a classroom, those errors must be revealed when students work on their homework and take quizzes and tests to receive feedback on their understanding.

Exercise: How anxious are you when making mistakes? How do you react to mistakes made by others? Do you think that your attitude

Self-satisfaction and delight

While working with my research students, I encourage them to search for their topics within specific subjects. Regardless of initial doubts about the validity of such topics, students work on their problems with great satisfaction. Satisfaction is the driving factor in long-term projects mentored outside of the classroom. In addition, it helps students find personal connections and additional meaning in their work.

The passion observed in students when they worked on research projects motivated my interest in the theories of creativity.

Regardless of initial resistance, students delight in working on creative assignments and observing others who work on such assignments with passion and delight. In STEM classrooms, passion may not be shared by many. Does creativity have enough force to transform STEM classroom into something more appealing?

Exercise: Do you feel delight when being creative? Is this feeling contagious? Do your students feel immense satisfaction when they are being creative? Do you think that such a feeling is essential in their future careers? Is it necessary for you in your career?

Assessments of the styles of facilitation

Taking constructive criticism is a part of the practice of creativity. Thus, collecting students' feedback regarding the creative assignments is necessary. Sometimes, specific details that disturb students may remain hidden in the eyes of the instructor. When introducing a class project, I usually give students six weeks to complete their work. However, after collecting a detailed survey, I found that students suggested announcing project topics and guidelines earlier during the semester to provide more time for thinking about the choice of topics and the creative aspects. Following this suggestion, during the following semesters, I announced the project topics within the first month of the classes, presented sample assignments from previous semesters, and shared videos with students' presentations. With the presenters' permission, I took videos of their presentations to share with future students. I always chose the most delighted and cheerful presenters, hoping such a display would help manage public speaking anxiety. Based on students' surveys, that was the most common issue among the four skills (writing, communication, and public speaking, mathematics skills, and collaborative skills) addressed during projects. However, my classes are full of non-native speakers; thus, a different skill may be the most challenging in another college and another course.

Sensitivity of creative process

The theory brought by Wallas (Wallas, 1926) and later discussed by multiple psychology and philosophy authors is not entirely aligned with the modern theories of Inquiry-Based Learning. However, it assumes that the Preparation stage is experienced effortlessly and naturally. However, this first stage would not occur without initial intentions for learning, questions in mind, or desires for discoveries. That is why the classrooms may be filled with students who have no curiosity and are not ready for the Preparation stage. However, the other stages will not take place without a proper approach to the preparation stage.

If the cycle of creative stages functions properly, it brings a sequence of satisfying events of inquiry, preparation, incubation, illumination, and verification, followed by more inquiry, etc. However, if the cycle does not function, where shall we address the difficulty as teachers and mentors?

Before responding to this question, one must observe that a deep inquiry is a subconscious stage, just like the stages of Incubation and Illumination. Thus, the creation process is an internal discussion between conscious and subconscious states. When the cycle does not work, one would like to find methods of addressing the difficulty.

Wallas mentions the mental tension between the conscious and subconscious (page 34) and points out that H. Poincaré already discussed this phenomenon in Science and Method. (Poincaré, 1914), who calls the force *'sensibilite'* translated as *'feeling.'* Is this feeling that needs to be addressed in the classroom when students experience difficulties solving problems or paying attention? Wallas, however, gives little hope for investigating methods of successful improvement of the creation process in terms of doing more or working harder. He even indicates that being more conscientious of the thinking process may disturb the thoughts and produce no results.

Thus, it is crucial to find what factors motivate and what demotivate creative thought for you and your students. Creative fluids are sensitive to disturbances, and unsuitable environments can ruin the creative process. The same environment may be encouraging and stimulating for one person but discouraging for another. All stages must work in unison for the creative thought to appear and be suitable for further development. If one stage does not work correctly due to certain internal or external circumstances, then all other stages may malfunction, giving the wrong impression that the entire cycle is limping. While working with your creative and professional creative activities, observe which stages flow smoothly and which are clumsy. Here are a handful of reasons why creativity may not flow, and for each, there is a stage affected by the given issue.

Insufficient or unstructured knowledge

It is subtle to realize that unstuffing knowledge is required to solve a problem, but it is even more subtle to know how to fill such a gap. When thinking about students learning basic skills in mathematics, I imagine they cannot learn more or learn better because the knowledge simply does not stick in their minds, and they cannot just put it there even if they want to very badly. In such a case, the preparation stage is not completed correctly.

The issue may run even more profoundly and may consist of not recalling the knowledge when it is needed. This results from the knowledge not being structured to provide a frame of associations. Moreover, that is the creative thought to bring the structure to the knowledge. I believe the repetitive process of increasing and structuring learned material may be helpful in such a case. This has already been discussed in previous chapters, together with the Bloom Taxonomy.

One can use road maps and visualizations of the known things in the form of a graph as a remedy. Sometimes, a table summarizing known, unknown, and impossible can work miracles. Some time ago, I worked with my collaborator on a project. While on the bus, I pulled notes with our work and looked where we had been stuck for a long time. Then, I placed all the known and unknown things on a table to make a summary and search for patterns, but I had no insight. When my collaborator later asked whether I had made any progress. I answered negatively but mentioned the table prepared on the bus. He immediately noticed an apparent mathematical structure when he looked at it, which I could not verbalize even if I felt something important there. Later, this structure became a topic of our paper. We still have not solved those problems where we were stuck before but placing the known and the unknown on a table led to a new opening and insight.

Weak imagination

It is a well-known story of David Hilbert's comment about a student who quit a math group to become a poet. Hilbert reacted with relief, claiming that the student had insufficient imagination to become a mathematician. This story may be plain rudeness of STEM towards humanities and arts. However, it carries the specific, not obvious, truth that creative work in STEM requires much vivid imagination placed on the edge of the impossible. Without deep imagination, the Incubation stage is not completed with suitable intensity. This story reminds me of my collaboration with students. When working on the solar panels in outer space projects, we could write science-fiction stories about all the impossible things we discuss during our regular research meetings. Such silly things do not appear in the scientific articles we publish in peer-reviewed journals. However, our thinking processes pass through impossible and unrealistic concepts daily. In my understanding, such an attitude of embracing the impossible is necessary when discussing hypothetical usages of nonexistent objects. Recalling a project with students, where they designed the lunar base, I realize that not knowing the environment on the moon, the equipment, the energy consumption, and the entire base organization, we have created a mind simulation of an entirely new reality. We visualized non-existent objects and their performance to interact with them and make calculations for them. Since we visited that reality frequently, our energy solidified to the point where we could hear, smell, and feel the objects we imagined.

As a remedy for weak imagination, I would suggest re-reading books and re-watching movies from one's childhood. There is a lot of encoded impossibility there waiting to be unpacked.

Lack of relaxation

Often overworked and fatigued, we forget that thinking is a relatively recent development in human evolution, and we are not entirely skillful while using this tool. Anybody with a headache or a migraine from overwhelming thinking understands the trouble. One must learn to stop thinking, relax, and forget about current work. It is like teaching a dog to run and then teaching it to stop running. Without skillful relaxation, the Incubation stage is not completed with refined energy but may create fatigue and restlessness.

Many of my classmates reported issues while studying when I was a student. Sitting at the desk to work on the assignments, we felt sleepy and lifeless. Then, when we would lie down to rest, we were suddenly awakened with memories of the lectures that came alive in vivid images and sounds. As a young mathematics student, I would go to the gym every day after studying to work out heavily. Without heavy-duty exercise, I could not rest, sleep, or work since my mind kept tirelessly recalling the topics from the lectures and the recitations. Without the capacity to stop thinking, I was often tired of excessive mind activities. I could not sleep or rest appropriately without disturbing thoughts. Fortunately, the practice of meditation brought some discipline to the mind. Now I can rest undisturbed. Thus, my mind is always fresh and ready to pick up on a new idea or project.

Various meditation techniques can come in handy for learning how to stop thinking. One can sing a mantra when disturbing thoughts arrive, habitually practice feeling one's own body, or learn to place one's mind in the state of questioning using Koan. The benefits of such a practice can be tremendous.

Insufficient connection between conscious and subconscious mind

It is like the inability to express someone's feelings. Even if a deep sense of knowing is available, it must be verbalized to communicate with others. The weak connection may result in a poor stage of Illumination. I believe communication among various parts of the mind plays a crucial role in developing a creative mind. This may be the proper place to provide some techniques for creating connections between the conscious and the subconscious mind. To recall, the conscious mind is responsible for short-term memory, critical and logical thinking, and free will. At the same time, the subconscious mind contains (but certainly is not limited to) long-term memory, intuition, imagination, emotions, and beliefs. To encourage building connections between those two minds, one could combine their activities, such as performing mechanical writing, painting, or drawing, and later intellectually analyze their meaning. Spontaneous doodling can reveal multiple patterns from the subconscious. My best method is writing down the dreams and then "honoring" them. To "honor" the dream, one can look up the meanings of the symbols that appear in the dream, draw the dream, or simply make one's way of admitting that the dream took place. You can look through the window thinking, "Now I am looking through the window to honor my dream," which encourages the connection between conscious and subconscious.

The problem with the conscious mind is that even if it takes only a few percent of our cognition (the tip of the iceberg), it "thinks" to be the majority of it. Making the first connection step with the subconscious may be enough to admit its existence, give it space, and then acknowledge its activities.

Fearing the moment of insight

It is an excellent mystery about humans that we frequently confront learning opportunities with fear rather than mystery and wonder. We seem to feel better when we know rather than when we learn. We defend our biases, beliefs, and storehouses of knowledge rather than inviting the unknown, the creative, and the inspirational. Being specific and closed gives us comfort while being doubtful and open gives us fear. The highest form of thinking we will ever learn is the humility of knowing that and what we do not know.

Fearing insight (or, on the other side, waiting for it impatiently) may disturb the subtle flow of energy throughout the creative stages. The reasons for fearing that moment may be multifold and may result from, for example, fear of changes that may follow the discovery, closely related to the fear of the unknown. In general, any strong emotion could override the flow of creative thought and disturb the sensitive stage of Illumination.

Healing the fears of the entire human population is a topic far beyond the scope of this work. However, in case of mild fears, one could try to work through them by meditation and exercise. Encourage acceptance and approval of the processes of the mind.

Exercise: How do you experience the moments of insight? Is it a joyful or painful experience? Do you think that this experience will change when you progress on the path of creative thinking?

High expectations combined with self-deprecation

A frequent reason for not growing creative thought properly is harsh judgment. Expecting instantaneous and perfect results combined with low skills may result in not picking up imperfect solutions or thoughts. This may be partially due to the typical stereotype of genius ideas appearing in a gifted mind or partially due to self-deprecation. As a result, the Verification stage does not develop properly.

When discussing free creative thoughts of children, we realize that their expectations and skills are very low. However, the lack of expectations allows children to try things simply. As we grow, the ego expands, carrying paralyzing self-doubt. This difficulty can be attacked twofold. One way is to eliminate the high expectations and perform creative activities for fun. The other way is to address self-deprecation by carefully questioning what matters to you. Instead of criticizing yourself, encourage constructive discussion of your flaws and virtues. This requires a connection with the subconscious.

Exercise: Identify the weakest stages of your creative thought. Can you see the reasons? Can you find simple remedies? It may be wise to strengthen all stages, whether they appear weak or strong. How would you strengthen the stages of creative thought?

Self-doubt

STEM teachers keep in mind that to teach STEM fields, one needs to master the topics. Indeed, teaching "integration by part" requires at least basic knowledge of the skills in integration, the method, and communication skills. However, is it reasonable to think similarly about teaching creativity? Do we need to feel creative enough to teach creativity? As STEM teachers, can we develop our creativity sufficiently to teach our students to be creative? Or is this task hopeless from the point of view of our logical STEM thinking?

You may not admit this publicly, but do you believe that only the best students should be taught creativity? Moreover, you do not include yourself among those exceptionally talented who deserve such honors? Since these deep beliefs may be obstacles to your successful implementation of the methods presented here, it would be worthwhile to reflect on them. In their paper, Paek and Sumners (Paek & Sumners, 2017) discuss how teachers' mindset affects their teaching of creativity.

To explain their work in a few sentences, one could say that teachers displaying fixed frames of mind did not appear as appealing examples of creative mindsets to their students, unlike teachers who displayed a flexible, open mind. Teaching creativity may be challenging for educators who enjoy their role as passive carriers of knowledge instead of active contributors. Being a STEM teacher who teaches known paths of inquiry and repetitive, schematic solutions, one may find this role of passive carrier very appealing. Introducing creativity in your classes is not about making sudden revolutionary changes and breaking all existing and comfortable thinking schemes. It is rather about learning and incorporating new tools where they make a good fit.

One of the features of the creative mind is seeing analogies in areas or situations that may be entirely unrelated. Here is an example of such an analogy. Some aspects of Martial Arts practice require learning and repeating forms prepared by others. The forms are sequences of attacking and defending moves, usually punches, blocks, and kicks, but sometimes locks or holds, depending on the style. Not all those sequences are simple and natural for all body types. With practice, I realized that if a move did not come out correctly, the fault was usually in the previous move(s). Moreover, that is the case for the stages of creativity. Having issues with **one single stage can be addressed by improving other stages.**

Exercise: Compare learning the stages of creative thought to another activity you do. What advice would you give yourself to improve that activity? Can this advice be applied to learning creative thinking?

In the light of developmental frameworks

According to developmental theories by Kegan (Kegan, 1982) or Dąbrowski (Dąbrowski, 1937) the stages of painful growth are alternated with stages of possibly peaceful plateaus. Thus, being held in the growth stage for a long time is not in the interest of the growing mind. Thus, three reasons come to mind as a reason for such a case:

1. Holding on to the old self. It may be challenging to let the old self go. It is almost like saying farewell to a friend or grieving a dying family member. However, this old self must go to allow the transformation. Some traditions or rituals may indicate sentiments toward the old self. Indeed, an environment may also hold to the old self, not allowing a smooth transition into a new self.

2. Fearing the unknown of the transitioning. Especially with a strong need for control, one can fear the transitions when the old self is already giving in, but the new self is not fully grown yet. This is a time of vulnerability and lacks the main features of a well-grown ego. It is being indecisive, lacking self-authority and self-trust. It may take a "safe space" to complete the transition smoothly. Otherwise, the transition may take longer and be particularly painful.

3. Failing to embrace the new self. That self may feel like a stranger, and it may be challenging to see its potential when the self is still "young." Not trusting anything that is not the previous "me" or not believing in the possibility of change, especially at a mature age, may be a reason for not accepting the new self as a new reality.

Reaching the Source

Too many steps have been taken.
returning to the root and the source.
Better to have been blind and deaf
from the beginning!
Dwelling in one's true abode,
unconcerned with and without -
The river flows tranquilly on
and the flowers are red

—9—

Reflections

There was no other time than the pandemic when creativity researchers flourished. As a journal editor, I have seen multiple submissions about creativity within the same semester when the pandemic began. Clearly, Spring 2020 gave us, teachers and students, a tough time but was unique and highly rewarding to those who knew how to take advantage of such circumstances. However, when the semester was over, it appeared that these times may be the most creative and "flowy" I ever experienced. During these weeks of solitude, I experienced high focus and delight in doing old things in new ways. Instead of being distracted by the commute, city activities, or meeting friends, I was able to circulate my thoughts around the classes. What was the charm? Was it solitude? The focus? Lack of other activities? Or the urgent necessity of the moment? The self-assessment of my classes was assisted by feedback from students received in the form of a mid-term survey. The semester when we suddenly converted our in-person classes to remote mode proved particularly productive and valuable for my creativity research.

Doing old things in new ways

In my understanding, trying old things in new ways provides an excellent opportunity for creative ideas that can be verified through a deliberate and repetitive feedback process. Throughout the semester, I had a chance to test new teaching ideas for remote learning. The first step was easy due to my extensive use of a writing stylus and communication apps like Zoom. During the first day of remote classes, which was incredibly stressful for my colleagues, I simply logged in to Zoom, opened a writing app, and lectured. I recorded the lectures, watched the recording, and immediately realized that my performance during remote teaching required significant improvements. However, two things made me happy: first of all, I knew that the recordings would give me neutral feedback, and second of all, I knew that due to the urgent change of the teaching modality, I would not be judged for not being perfect. With these two things in mind, I have begun reflecting on how to develop my new remote teaching style through trial and error.

Constant feedback from students and recorded class videos

After watching the videos a few times, I quickly observed that the sound quality was insufficient for uninterrupted attention. My students kept notifying me that the sound went on and off. I realized it was due to my rocking and grabbing my tablet's microphone. To improve that, I tried to use a headset, but it did not help since I got entangled in the cord, and then I realized the sound quality got even worse because the microphone from my cellphone headset did not catch my voice well. I ended up buying a professional microphone suitable for the timbre of my voice. Since that time, the quality of the recordings has significantly improved, and I did not hear any complaints from my students.

The quality of the videos proved to be much trickier to improve. I was sure that my handwriting was legible, and the quality of the screen was very high; however, when I asked my students during a survey whether they could see the screen well, many of them said that on their screens, my handwriting appeared very small, and they cannot see it well. To respond to this issue, I enlarged my screen. However, it took until the end of the semester for me to realize the actual problem. Depending on the spread of my notes, I positioned my tablet vertically or horizontally. However, the view on my students' screens did not adjust similarly. If their position was horizontal and mine was vertical, then their view had two dark stripes on the sides, and my vertical screen would have been much smaller than my view. When I realized that, I simply flipped my tablet horizontally (even if it was not always the most convenient position to keep my notes displayed) and did not change it. Without students' feedback, I would have never figured out why they could not see my screen in its proper enlargement.

Two-sided respect and appreciation

Throughout the semester, my students and I kept exchanging signs of respect and appreciation. I asked my students whether they are staying safe, healthy and sane during each class. My students kept asking the same questions to me. One of my students expressed her appreciation to all her teachers because she thought converting entire courses into a remote mode in just a few days was laborious. Every day, when I felt moody, I thought that I could not crash mentally because I had to be there for my students. They were waiting for me, looking forward to quality instruction delivered professionally.

During one of my office hours, the wife of my student came to the camera and said that her husband likes my class very much and talks about it all the time. That student said he dislikes online classes and dropped out of other courses but stays in my class because he likes the teaching style. I felt very empowered by these statements and was even more motivated to improve my lectures. Another student who met me during office hours emphasized asking students to fill out a survey, which was significant to her. She felt anonymous while hiding behind her computer screen, but the survey gave her a voice.

There are still lots of things to develop and improve

I have no doubts that remote teaching is different from teaching in person. It requires different approaches and different assessments. There is still much work to do to improve my remote teaching style. I thought I could look through some YouTube videos of lectures and get inspired by them.

So far, my biggest concern is designing exams that minimize academic dishonesty. In exam problems, I am trying to bring a flow of exercises that start with basic skills, progress to more complicated tasks, and conclude with some written statements of explanations. In my understanding, problems that offer a combination of drawing, writing, and math skills are suitable for remote exams.

Challenges: Falling into a routine of working around the clock

As I heard from my colleagues, some fell into laziness, and some fell into routines of working around the clock. I was in the second group. Having a delightful line of inquiry related to my work and having no motivation to stop working, no meeting friends, no concerts, museums, or exhibitions, I fell into the routine of working from early morning till late evening. This lifestyle was enjoyable for a few weeks, but I quickly realized I was becoming less efficient and less motivated. At that moment, I run into another book by Csiksentmihalyi (Csiksentmihalyi, 1974) about creating a schedule that facilitates flow. Inspired by his work and again delighted by the idea of doing something new, I began experimenting with my schedule by introducing walks, listening to audiobooks, and combining other activities with intelligent multitasking.

Thus, I developed activities such as doing the dishes while listening to casual books and exercising during meetings, where I did not have to show my face. This led me to further improvements in my home office by "proofreading" documents and listening to them with the "Read out Loud." This way, I could catch typos invisible to my eyes, such as "form" instead of "from." They look alike but sound so different. I used this option before but did not find typos in my documents. Thus, to avoid working around the clock, I started reflecting on and improving my work schedule and working style. This led me to schedule walks and times for artwork and stay in touch with friends. Eventually, I could leave the vicious circle of working around the clock.

Midterm survey and students' responses

After searching for suitable questions and consulting with my colleagues, I prepared a mid-term survey via SurveyMonkey. Here are the questions asked to students. Some questions may seem plain but placing them in the survey yielded unexpected results.

1. Are you experiencing any difficulties or challenges? With yourself, family members, or friends?
2. Describe your access to a computer and a WIFI network. Can you use them freely? Have you experienced any difficulties?
3. Do you hear the lecture well? Is my microphone working well? Are your speakers working well?
4. Do you see the lecture well? Is my camera working well? Is your screen clear, large, and bright enough to provide a comfortable view?

5. Are you receiving my messages? Did you open the OneNote document? Did you watch the video recording from our class posted on Dropbox?

6. Do you think any policies in our course (homework, grading, etc.) should be changed? I cannot promise to take your advice, but I will consider it very seriously.

7. Is there anything about our course that you particularly like? As we make changes, I want to ensure we preserve what is best about our course and to build on it potentially.

8. Have you attended our virtual classes life, via the recordings, or not at all? Describe your experience, primarily what has worked for you and what has been more challenging.

9. Do you feel comfortable participating in our course? Is there anything I could do to make you feel more comfortable participating?

10. Can you share strategies you have used to adjust to distance learning that have worked for you that I should recommend to other students? Please describe these strategies. Alternatively, you can describe strategies that have not worked for you and what you plan to do differently after the break.

The response rate in my two classes was about 50%. For the first question, most responders reported no difficulties or challenges. However, a few mentioned difficulties with staying focused at home and overcoming the temptation to visit social media, which is "one click away." Some reported losses in family and illnesses, which escalated as the semester progressed. To my surprise, nobody reported difficulties with Wi-Fi or computer access. As expected, most students complained about the sound quality, but unexpectedly, few mentioned that the writing was too small for them to read on their screens.

Since the class syllabus did not require attending all class meetings and recommended watching the videos in case of missing classes, I expected mixed answers to the question about watching videos. Similarly, since opening class notes in OneNote requires some software skills and not all students have the patience to deal with stubborn software, I expected varied answers to that part of the survey. Regarding course policies, some students asked for more quiz time, and some asked for more class time. Students appreciated access to the recordings and my willingness to answer questions during lectures. Some students mentioned that they prefer remote classes because previously, they had a long commute and difficulties paying attention in a classroom since they felt distracted, among others.

Encouraging and monitoring students' participation in remote synchronous classes has been challenging throughout the semester. This challenge was the motivation for question 9 of the survey. Students' answers varied as much as their behavior in class. The group of responders split into three equal subgroups, with some students claiming that they feel comfortable, some that they do not, and some that they do not know. One response pointed out that answering questions via chat and sending them only to me, instead of the entire class, was way more comfortable than sending a message to everybody. I concluded that encouraging private messaging may be the way to approach this challenge of students' participation in remote synchronous classes. In addition, students earn "activity" points by responding to my questions, but this is not a new idea since I used it previously in my classes to give credit to students who solved problems on the board.

The most exciting part of the survey came from students answering the last question about their tips for studying in the new learning mode. Some students had no suggestions or tips, but some apparently got creative in dealing with new circumstances and described their methods in long responses. One student mentioned that he studies by following the examples of the videos and watching them multiple times. Another suggested making a list of things to do and then pacing himself on the progress. Someone said: "wake up early to get things done" and "split up work instead of doing it all at once". One student wrote:

"I had to be extremely punctual and ensure I was on Blackboard or ready to get on Zoom 10 minutes earlier. I started checking my email and Blackboard announcements very frequently. I made a calendar, and I wrote 'Post. It is reminders everywhere, so I remember what I am scheduled to do."

Another student said that he keeps no lights in a dark room when he studies, with the only light coming from the monitor and the keyboard. This helps him focus and avoid distractions since he sees nothing around.

Someone mentioned creating a habit of daily studies to avoid accumulating stress, which would add to life stress. Another person reviews the class material before attending the lecture to "get tuned" to the course. All these suggestions were constructive, and I could apply them to myself.

Exercise: The time of the pandemic was challenging yet rewarding. How do you handle new challenges? What did you learn about yourself, your colleagues, and your students? How would you prepare if you knew another pandemic would occur in 2, 5, or 10 years? Would you pile up more food, buy a new computer, or develop new skills? What kind of skills? Creativity skills?

Return to Society

Barefooted and naked of breast,
I mingle with the people of the world.
My clothes are ragged and dust-laden,
and I am ever blissful.
I use no magic to extend my life;
Now, before me, the dead trees
become alive

Epilogue

Writing this book assisted me through many life events: moving in and out, renovating, tearing the walls down and putting them up, taking care of a family member, losing a family member, breaking up, and falling in love. Every time, even if the writing flow was lost, I kept returning to writing, finding the flow repeatedly and asking myself this question over and over: Why do I even need to write a book? This book? Moreover, why do I need to finish it? Many ideas came and faded in the writing process, but quite a few remained. I wanted to write because I have experienced something valuable and want to share it with others. The writing itself helped me reflect on this experience in an organized way so my understanding of the process could crystallize and clarify. Regardless of enjoying the process of looking inward and writing, I have realized that at some point, it all has to come to an end, and the book must be finished. One can formulate many good reasons for finishing writing a book. For example, the book is complete, or ideas for other books are already chiming into the author's mind. I re-wrote this book many times when my reflections changed my views on multiple topics. Honestly, I am thankful to the book for staying with me patiently during the creation process and for not complaining about multiple changes and turns of ideas. The book taught me to organize myself, make commitments, break commitments, apologize, and return to commitments.

Looking back and reflecting forward, I wish to know more about how people generally encourage and grow their creativity. Having this certainty of various approaches, I know that every person has their unique way and needs to follow their unique path to grow and flourish. However, at the same time, I know that we pass the same milestones and cross the same mountain passes on that path. Thus, by knowing the trace of each path, we could approximate the shape of the mountain.

Gshiselin (Ghiselin, 1952) presents a collection of first-hand descriptions of the creative process from a variety of the best authors and thinkers from the past. It is heart-warming to know that other people experience creative vibes, observe them, and write books about them.

Being on a (creative) journey is already a creative act of the self, as mentioned in (Lengyel, 1971). He points out that we all have the potential for creative skills to create ourselves. However, meeting someone who took that skill to perfection is rare. Once discussing the appearance of monks, someone stated that "they all look alike because they all have the same mind; they are one person." Thinking that they are performing the same tasks daily, one may expect that the monks will eventually appear alike, but when they began their journey, they did not look the same. This touches upon another topic: What practices can shape the mind profoundly and meaningfully?

The book may end here, but my mind keeps working on creating new ideas, possibly for future assignments.

Could awakening creativity be aligned with dominant cognitive functions?

This topic has fascinated me since I began analyzing the cognitive functions of my students, family, and friends. The existing tests do not necessarily address the "study personality type" displayed by students at the school or a college but provide some approximation. Keeping in mind that my students need different ways of learning, I see a need to know their types of learning. Some students are visual, some learn by doing physical models with their hands, some learn by abstract concepts, and some learn while teaching others. Similarly, I imagine learning creative skills goes through various paths for various people. My next idea is to collect written reports of developing creativity, with all challenges (resolved or not) and pains and try to match them with the Myers-Briggs personality types.

Could we design machines that are creative in a meaningful way?

This question is on the boundary of artificial intelligence and science fiction. As an educator, I would say yes, we need to raise a generation of scientists who will think creatively and have the capacity to observe themselves so insightfully that the products of their work will be able to have the skills of creativity.

Or maybe the times of creative machines are not that far away from today? Designing a program that walks through the stages of creativity seems a step away from what we have now.

The theoretical foundations of such software are pretty straightforward and generally follow the idea of shifting between the conscious and subconscious mind. The conscious mind builds solid connections among the objects based on their meanings. These tight associations are necessary to define precise concepts, provide proof, use scientific methods, or pay salaries. However, the subconscious mind builds weak connections among the objects based on their geometrical shapes, smells, colors, sounds, or other associations that make no connections with the meaning; for example, things coincidentally happening at the same time may be subconsciously associated regardless of obvious nonsense of conscious relation. These weak and broad associations are crucial for solving problems, finding new applications of old things, and adjusting to new situations. In addition, expressing weak associations in certain forms (for example, music, dance, or poetry) shifts the mind to a different reality.

This question gets an entirely different expression after the launch of the AI-trained chatbots in November 2023. After the initial mix of feelings and feedback involving big laughs related to funny AI poems or photos, it becomes clear that AI will mark the following stages of human evolution. I hope for the better.

Is creativity and personal development an evolutionary direction?

Andre Lamier in (Lamier, 2012) discusses the development of the structures of the mind in light of the aging human population. Continuing the train of thought based on Kegan's Theory (Kegan, 1982) one could inquire about the influence of the order of the mind on aging and the quality of life of elderly people. I imagine in my abductive thinking that the interest and motivation for creative thought and personal development would significantly increase if someone justified that those who reach order 4 or 5 are immune to Alzheimer's disease Parkinson's disease or live longer and happier. Would the direction of the entire industry and society change due to a shift in the thinking that the quality of the cognitive functions of elderly people can only decline?

Carl Rogers, on page 196 (Rogers, 1959) quotes Andras Angyal:

"Life processes do not merely tend to preserve life, but transcend the momentary status quo of the organism, expanding itself continually and imposing its autonomous determination upon an ever-increasing realm of events."

Those words in my mind touch upon the magic of transforming the independent sums of every moment into cohesive memories that later

184

enrich every moment afterward. This has had a vast impact on the way I treat my current state of mind. I do not have much influence on them today, but I have an infinitesimal influence on what will come to my mind stream in the future. Piling up a lot of such infinitesimal experiences of creative thoughts can significantly improve the mind in the future.

Acknowledgements

I am grateful to Professor Bronisław Czarnocha for his endless energy, encouragement, multiple enlightening discussions, and this fantastic attitude of camaraderie and belonging.

Writing seminars I have attended proved extremely helpful in preparing, endlessly revising the drafts, and staying motivated while working. In particular, I am grateful to Professor Maria Jerskey for organizing the Literacy Brokers Writing Circle, for consistently supporting faculty writing efforts with the right spirit. In the meantime, I have searched for help scheduling writing sessions in various places. One was a meetup.com group of scholars and writers across the disciplines. Such groups' support proved crucial for keeping the motivation while completing and revising the manuscript.

Yes, it takes the whole village to write a book.

References

A Framework for Creative Insights Within Internalization. (2023). In *Ongoing Advancements in Philosophy of Mathematics Education* (pp. 183-208). Springer.

Ackerman, E., & et al. (1964). A Mathematical Model of the Glucose-tolerance test. *Phys. Med. Biol. 9 203*.

Alvarado, R., Averett, M., & et al. (2021). Game of Cycles. *Monthly, Mathematical Association of America*.

Anderson, L. W., & Krathwohl, D. R. (2001). *A Taxonomy for Learning, Teaching, and Assessing: A Revision of Bloom's Taxonomy of Educational Objectives.*

Barr, M. C., & et al. (2001). Direct monolithic integration of organic photovoltaic circuits on unmodified paper. *Advanced Materials*, 3499-3505.

Bear, M. F., Connors, B. W., & et al. (2006). *Neuroscience: Exploring the Brain*. Williams&Wilkins.

Bloodhart, B., & Balgopal, M. (2020). Outperforming yet undervalued: Undergraduate women in STEM. *PLOS ONE 15(6)*, 1-13.

Bloom, B. S., & Krathwohl, D. R. (1956). *Taxonomy of Educational Objectives: The Classification of Educational Goal*. Longman.

Cardoza, J., & Marciniak, M. (2024). *Influence of Light Color on the Mood and Perception*. Long Island City: Ad Astra Newsletter.

Chamberlin, S., Liljedahl, P., & Savich, M. (2022). *Mathematical Creativity: A developmental perspective*. Springer.

Chan Barrett, K., & Limb, C. J. (2019). Unveiling artistic minds: case studies of creativity. *Science Direct, Current Opinion in Behavioral Sciences, 27,* 84-89.

Cho, E., & et al. (2019). Numerical Estimation of Solar Resource for Curved Panels on Earth and Mars. *Proc SPIE 10913.*

Chowdhury, R., & et al. (2020). Optimization of solar cell packing models for flexible surfaces. *SPE 11275.*

Chowdhury, R., & Marciniak, M. (2019). Optimal geometry of solar cells with genetics algorithm. *SPIE 10913.*

Costa, A., & Kallick, B. (2000). The 16 Habits of Mind. *A Developmental Series. Association for Supervision and Curriculum Development:.*

Csikszentmihalyi, M. (1974). *Beyond Boredom and Anxiety: Experiencing Flow in Work and Play.* San Francisco: Josey-Bass.

Czarnocha, B., & Marciniak, M. (2023). Living in the ongoing moment. In M. Viggiani Bicudo, B. Czarnocha, M. Rosa, M. Marciniak, & (Editors), *Ongoing Advancements in Philosophy of Mathematics Education* (pp. 461-466). Springer Nature.

Dąbrowski, K. (1937). Psychological Basis of Self Mutilation. *Genetic Psychology Monographs 19,* 1-104.

Drago-Severson, E. (2004). *Becoming Adult Learners. Principles and Practice for Effective Development.* Teachers College Press.

Ellis, M. W., & Berry III, R. Q. (2005). The paradigm shift in mathematics education: explanations and implications of reforming conceptions of teaching and learning. *The Mathematics Educator, 15.*

Ford, J. (2018). Blended team-based learning with standard-base grading. *Mathematics Teaching-Research Journal vol10 no3-4,* 52-70.

Frawley, W. (1997). *Vygotsky and Cognitive Science: Language and the Unification of the Social and Computational Mind.* Harvard University Press.

Ghiselin, B. (1952). *The creative process. A symposium.* University of California Press.

Hackett, E., & et al. (1992). Industry, academe, and the values of undergraduate engineers. *Research in Higher Education. 33(3):,* 275-295.

Hassanpour, A. E., Slker, J. S., & Higgins, C. W. (2018). Remarkable agrivoltaics influence on soil moisture, micrometeorology, and water-use efficiency. *PLOS ONE 13(11).*

Hau, E. (2013). *Wind Turbines.* Berlin: Springer.

Joukowsky, N. E. (1912). Über die Konturen der Tragflächen der Drachenflieger. *Zeitschrift fur Flugtechnik und Motorluftschiffahrt 1, and 3,* 181-284, and 81-86.

Kawamoto, H., & et al. (2011). Mitigatiom of Lunar Dust on Solar Panels and Optical Elements Utilizing Electrostatic Traveling-Wave. *Science Direct.*

Kegan, R. (1982). *The Evolving Self.* Cambridge, England: Harvard University Press.

Keysers, C., Kaas, J. H., & Gazzola, V. (2010). Somatosensation in social perception. *Nat Rev Neurosci 11(6),* 417-28.

Koestler, A. (1964). *The Act of Creation.* Macmillan.

Kuhn, T. (2012). *The structure of scientific revolutions.* University of Chicago Press.

Lamier, A. (2012). Post-Formal Thought in Gerontagogy or beyond Piaget. *Journal of Behavioral and Brain Science, 2,* 399-406.

Laplace, P. (1812). *Théorie analytique des probabilités.* Paris: Courcier.

Lengyel, C. (1971). *The creative self.* The Netherlands: Mouton.

Majid, Z. A., Ruslan, M. H., Sopian, K., Othman, M. Y., & Azmi, M. S. (2014). Study on performance of 80mwatt floating photovoltaic panel. *Journal of Mechanical Engineering and Sciences 7(1),* 1150-1156.

Marciniak, M. (2020). Creativity during the time of pandemic. *Mathematics Teaching-Research Journal vol 12 no 1*, 3-8.

Marciniak, M. (2023). The times of transitions in the Modern Education. In M. Viggiani Bicudo, B. Czarnocha, M. Rosa, M. Marciniak, & (Editors), *Ongoing Advancements in Philosophy of Mathematics Education* (pp. 239-251). Springer Nature.

Marciniak, M. A. (2017). Minutes from math meetings with an undergraduate student. *Mathematics Teaching-Research Journal 9, 1-2*.

Marciniak, M. A., & et al. (2017). Efficiency of geometric designs of non-tracing flexible solar panels: mathematical simulation. *Proc SPIE 10379.*

Marciniak, M. A., Hassebo, Y., & et al. (2018). Efficient geometry of flexible solar panels optimized for the latitude of New York City. *Proc SPIE 10758.*

Marciniak, M. A., Nechayeva, M., Przhebelskiy, V., & et al. (2017). Green power statistics: local wind speed modeling as basis for wind turbine performance prediction;. *JSM Proceedings Section on Statistics and the Environment*, (pp. 2195-2199).

Margolis, H. (1987). *Patterns, thinking and cognition, A theory of judgment.* Chicago and London: The University of Chicago Press.

Marzenic, M. M. (2013). *Soft-wired : how the new science of brain plasticity can change your life.* San Francisco: Parnassus Pub.

Maskal, L., Aboudiwan, A., & Marciniak, M. A. (2020). Solar panels for the lunar base. *Proc SPIE 11275.*

May, R. (1975). *The courage to create.* New York: WW Norton Company, Inc.

May, R. (1975). *The courage to create.* New York: W W Norton & Company, INC.

McCarthy Gallager, J., & Reid, D. K. (2002). *The Learning Theory of Piaget and Inhelder.* iUniverse.

Mumaw, S., & Oldfield, W. (2006). *Caffeine for the creative mind: 250 exercises to wake up your brain.* Cincinnati, Ohio: HOW BOOKS.

Nadga, B. A., & et al. (1998). Undergraduate student-faculty research partnerships affect student retention. *Review of Higher Education. 22:*, 55-72.

Paek, S. H., & Sumners, S. E. (2017). The indirect effect of teacher's creative mindset on teaching creativity. *Journal of Creative Behavior, Publication of the Creative Education Foundation 53.3,* 298-311.

Pandya, R., & et al. (2018). Mathematical simulation of efficiency of various shapes of solar panels for NASA geostationary satellites. *Proc SPIE 10527.*

Parker, S., Traver, A., & Cornick, J. (2017). Contextualizing developmental math context into an introduction to sociology in community colleges. *CUNY Academic Commons.*

Piaget, J. (1952). *The Origins of Intelligence in Children.* New York: International Universities Press.

Pineda, J. A. (2009). *Mirror Neuron Systems: The Role of Mirroring Processes in Social Cognition.* Humana Press.

Poincaré, H. (1914). *Science and Method.*

Ramachandran, V. (1995). *Mirror Neurons and Imitation Learning as the Driving Force Behind the Great Leap Forward in Human Evolution.*

Rogers, C. R. (1959). *A Theory of Therapy, Personality, and Interpersonal Relationships: As Developed in the Client-centered Framework.* McGraw-Hill.

Rua, T., de Kortb, Y. A., & et al. (2019). Non-image forming effects of illuminance and correlated color temperature of office light on alertness, mood, and performance across cognitive domains. *Building and Environment 149*, 253-263.

Russell, S. H., & et al. (2007). The pipeline: Benefits of undergraduate research experience. *Science 316(5824),* 548-549.

Simmons, G. F. (2018). *Differential Equations with Applications and Historical Notes.* Chapman&Hall.

Steinhaus, H. (2024). *Między Duchem a Materią Pośredniczy Matematyka.* Warsaw: Wydawnictwo Naukowe PWN .

Taylor, J. M. (2016). *Mirror Neurons After a Quarter Century: New light, new cracks.*

Torres, D. E. (2018). The Student(s) Or How can I make this interesting? "It starts and ends with and experience". *Creativity in STEM* (pp. 48-49). The Bonx: Proceedings of the CUNY research summit.

van Torgeren, M. (2023). *Overtone Singing: Harmonic Dimensions of the Human Voice.*

Vartanian, O., Bristol, A., & Kaufman, J. (2013). *Neuroscience of creativity.* Cambridge, Massachusets: The MIT Press.

Viggiani Bicudo, M., Czarnocha, B., Rosa, M., & Marciniak, M. (2023). *Ongoing Advancements in Philosophy of Mathematics Education.* Springer Nature Switzerland.

Vygotsky, L. S. (1978). *Mind in Society: The Development of Higher Psychological Processes.* Cambridge, MA: Harvard University Press.

Wallas, G. (1926). *The Art of Thought.*

Weisberg, R. W., & Reeves, L. M. (2013). *Cognition. From Memory to Creativity.* Wiley & Sons.

Woodworth, R. S. (1938). *Experimental Psychology.* Holt.

www.ingramcontent.com/pod-product-compliance
Lightning Source LLC
Chambersburg PA
CBHW071714140626
46557CB00011B/132